PARANOIA TO POSSIBILITY

PARANOIA TO
POSSIBILITY

ESCAPE SMALL THINKING, LISTEN LIKE A MASTER, AND LEAD WITH YOUR BEST

AMIEL HANDELSMAN

Adam,
With the
deepest respect.

Amiel
11/7/2013

JZ LEADERSHIP PRESS

Published by JZ Leadership Press, Portland, OR

Amiel Handelsman, 1970-
Portland, OR
amiel@amielhandelsman.com
amielhandelsman.com

ISBN 978-0-9895895-0-5
First Edition

Cover by Sarah Heckles

Printed in the United States of America

To Ben Handelsman

CONTENTS

1 IN 10,000 CHANCE

"THAT'S IMPOSSIBLE! THE doctor said we had a one in ten thousand chance."

It was just past 10 a.m. in Portland, and I was standing in the bathroom next to my wife. She had just pulled me out of a post-brunch conversation I was having in our living room with two friends. With a radiant smile on her face, she held up a small test strip showing a "plus" sign.

"Look, Amiel," she replied. "It's right there. This means we're pregnant."

"Julie, that line looks faint. It can't be right. One in ten thousand chance. Do you really think we are that one?"

She smiled.

I realized then that I wasn't going to win this argument even though I was obviously right. And she *was* glowing. What business did I have spoiling such an uplifting moment, however misconstrued? So I took a deep breath, said, "Well, let's hope so," gave her a kiss, and returned to our friends.

Eight months later, our son, Jacob, was born.

That was the first inspiration for writing a book about opening your mind and heart to possibility.

After "Aha!" Comes...?

THE SECOND INSPIRATION for this book came a year later in a conference room of a large corporation. Steve (a pseudonym) and I were sitting across the table from each other. This was our first meeting, and he had an important question for me.

"Look," he said. "I've been working here for 15 years, and I've been to a lot of leadership classes. The one I went to last month was far and away the best, particularly the part about possibility thinking. That's not how we usually do things here, so it had a big impact on me—almost hard to describe. When I walked out, I felt like something had changed in me. But then I got back into the job here..." He paused and gulped. "Well, let's just say it's been hard to maintain that same excitement. My days are very full. There's a lot of pressure. So... how do you suggest I keep it going?"

"What in particular would you like to keep going?" I asked.

"I need to focus on what's possible rather than what's wrong. Listening to people rather than just arguing with them. This could make a big difference in my group, and I have to lead the way. Can you help me?"

"Yes, I can help you," I replied.

And that is what I proceeded to do—not only with Steve, but with fifteen other managers in his company. All of them had taken the same seminar and experienced a powerful "aha" moment unlike any they had experienced before. And all of them were finding it difficult to extend that moment into an ongoing lived reality. What they really wanted was confirmation from their own experience that what they saw in that seminar—a new way of leading, indeed a new way of living—was real. Not an error or aberration, but something that could produce tangible results in a company of hard-nosed people.

It was almost as though these managers were showing me a pregnancy test strip with a plus sign that indicated "possible" rather than "pregnant." They wanted to believe that this plus sign was accurate because it would mean a new way of experiencing life. However, they had been around the block long enough to hold this faith lightly, and they were unclear how to start.

In reality, their leadership journey had already started... and then been sidetracked. My job as their coach was not only to help them get back on track, but also to reframe what the journey was about and what it would take to complete it.

I call this the journey from paranoia to possibility. *Paranoia* is a strong word that I use to describe not these managers as individuals but a key piece of the organizational culture in which they learned to manage. This quality shows up in several ways: conversations in which people critique what's wrong with ideas rather than explore what's right, fear-based control systems that waste time and drain human energy, and performance management approaches that foster unhealthy competition at the expense of collaboration.

These managers faced two main challenges:

- How do you lead people to explore new possibilities and trust each other when the culture has historically discouraged these things?

- Once you've developed a new approach to leadership, how do you use it to transform this very culture?

These challenges—and the larger journey from paranoia to possibility—are not unique to the sixteen managers at this company. In my twenty years developing leaders, I've seen them show up in countless places, from Fortune 100 companies to professional service firms to large health care systems to government agencies to relatively small not-for-profit organizations. Not every organization has a paranoid culture, but many do, and every one that does is filled with managers looking for a better way to lead.

I've written this book for all of these managers.

Perhaps one of them is you.

Sneak Preview

THIS BOOK IS a how-to guide with an edge. The edge arises from three beefs I have with many popular leadership books:

1. They claim to show you how to become a better leader, but don't provide actionable recommendations. *Actionable* means that it's physical; you can capture it on videotape. Giving leaders actual phrases to incorporate into questions is actionable. Instructing them to ask better questions is not. This book provides phrases.

2. They emphasize leaders' outer behaviors and ignore their thoughts, feelings, and worldviews. This book provides both outer and inner practices of possibility leadership.

3. They treat all leaders the same. Ever read a book instructing you to be "bolder?" I'm all for boldness, but for many leaders this isn't the most important quality to cultivate. In fact, I've worked with leaders who are bold to a fault. They need to learn to pause

and consider the impact of their decisions before acting. This book assumes that different leaders have different needs.

This book is organized to provide answers to two questions:

- Why would you want to take the journey to possibility leadership?

- How would you do this, from who you are now, within the organization where you work?

Part One answers the *why* question. Parts Two, Three, and Four answer the *how* question. By the time you're finished, you may be asking the *who* question: if you step fully into possibility leadership and transform how you speak, listen, and think, who could you become?

Part One begins with the idea that, yes, there is an upside to paranoia, but only when used consciously and selectively rather than impulsively and universally. Even then, it cannot compete with the downside of paranoia, which I illustrate through the examples of managing performance through forced ranking, requiring face time, and over-scheduling. Just when you think I'm about to swing a sledgehammer at all advocates of paranoid leadership, I examine the ideas of one such advocate and find much to admire. After a quick preview of the contours of possibility leadership, I ask, "To what end?" and "Where will you focus?"

At this point, if you're still excited by the possibility of possibility leadership, you'll find in Parts Two and Three a specific set of practices for becoming this kind of leader—not just when it's convenient, but all of the time.

Part Two contains eight practices that are visible to others, so I call them "outer" practices:

- I describe how trying to find a girlfriend taught me about *conversations for possibility*, and how specifically to design and hold these kinds of conversations in your organization. (Chapter 7)

- I invite you to pay close attention to the hundreds of "micro-interactions" you have each day. You will see why *turning toward* other people in these micro-interactions builds trust, why turning away from and turning against others doesn't, and how to turn toward others more consistently. (Chapter 8)

- If all of this turning doesn't leave you too dizzy—or if it does and you start complaining about it—you'll enjoy the next challenge: taking your everyday complaints seriously. Not by believing them, but by finding within them the signs of what matters most to you. *Flipping these complaints* and publicly declaring the commitments you discover within them has great potential to positively affect the mood of your team and organization. This flip isn't something you learned in school, so I provide a five-step approach to carrying it out. (Chapter 9)

- After providing an amusing recipe for mediocre arguing, I offer five suggestions for how to *argue better*. For example, by distinguishing assessments from factual assertions and asking others to ground their assessments; in short: by not being an arrogant know-it-all. (Chapter 10)

- I describe why *storytelling* is a powerful leadership tool and suggest resources for developing your competence at this. (Chapter 11)

- After challenging popular notions about listening, I reveal the secrets of *listening like a master*. For example, what specifically gets in the way of your listening well to others? (Chapter 12)

- I describe why *asking* "dumb" *questions* is smart and offer specific "power phrases" you can use to make your dumb questions even dumber. This section alone is worth the price of the book, and that's before we get into the mood and intention behind your questions. Words aren't everything! (Chapter 13)

- Part Two concludes with a five-point scale for assessing the quality of your relationships and determining which are truly pivotal to your success. After reading my suggestions for improving relationships, you'll have a very different understanding of what it means to *neutralize enemies*. (Chapter 14)

Part Three introduces seven "inner" practices of possibility leadership. These practices are all real, tangible things you can do that others may or may not see, depending upon where you do them:

- I describe what Kirk Gibson can teach us about *visualizing* big possibilities and how you can do this yourself. Hint: start with, "Wouldn't it be great if____?" (Chapter 15)

- Stories about Intel and Honda remind us that many of the best strategies are not deliberate but emergent. Strategies emerge when you learn how to recognize patterns of behavior from the past, such as market shifts and how your middle managers respond to them. This skill of *seeing patterns* will also allow you to spot hidden strengths in your team. (Chapter 16)

- I introduce nine distinctive *"Achilles Heels."* One is likely a source of vulnerability for you that can be healed. (Chapter 17)

- Then I take this a step further by challenging you to *"call B.S."* on *yourself*—and, yes, I even spell out what those initials stand for. Parental advisory encouraged. (Chapter 18)

- I acknowledge how difficult it is to take on new practices when life is already full. This leads to tips on how to create a trusted system for *managing commitments*: all the projects, activities, and actions that matter to you. And the stuff that doesn't matter? Enter "Dumpster Days" at stage left. (Chapter 19)

- I focus on one topic that is so important it is rarely mentioned in any leadership book: how to *manage your physical energy* to meet the extraordinary demands of being a manager. I share the best lessons my clients have used in the areas of sleeping, exercise, nutrition, and renewal. (Chapter 20)

- With your attention now focused on your body, I invite you to consider your body *posture*—what it is, and the enormous impact it has on your mood and your openness to possibility. (Chapter 21)

Part Four is about how to practice possibility leadership. It describes what you can learn about the process of practicing from competitive athletes, elite musicians, and performing artists. And, how this might translate into tangible methods of practice in your organization:

- I describe the attributes of *deliberate practice* and four ways to do this directly: the music approach, the chess approach, the sports conditioning approach, and the sports simulation approach. You'll realize that you already know everything you need to know about how to practice. What's left to do is employ this knowledge in a new context. (Chapter 22)

- I introduce a four-step *on-the-job practice cycle*. I discuss how to *prepare* your mind and body before you *act*, give you specific questions you can use to *reflect* afterwards (and show you how you know you are making progress in becoming more competent at reflecting), and discuss the attributes of high-quality *feedback* and how you can ensure that you are receiving it. (Chapter 23)

- I ask you to consider what *challenging experiences* will help you grow and how to get these experiences in either your current job or a new job. (Chapter 24)

- Part Four concludes with stories of three people who have made the leap from practicing possibility leadership to integrating it into their *way of being*. (Chapter 25)

   Paranoia to Possibility includes stories from my own experience to remind you—and me—that we are all learning about this topic together.

Amiel Handelsman
amiel@amielhandelsman.com
Portland, Oregon
June 18, 2013

PARANOIA TO POSSIBILITY

PART ONE

WHY POSSIBILITY LEADERSHIP?

CHAPTER 1

THE PROMISE OF PARANOIA

"IT IS NOT change that causes anxiety; it is the feeling that we are without defenses in the presence of what we see as danger that causes anxiety."
—Robert Kegan and Lisa Laskow Lahey, *Immunity to Change*[1]

This is the chapter where I establish my street credibility with you.

If you're reading this book, it's likely that you have experience with managing people in a paranoid culture and, quite possibly, have risen into the executive ranks. As a result, when you see the title *Paranoia to Possibility*, you may wonder two things:

1. Does this author understand the benefits of approaching the future with prudence and restraint, or does he expect me to trade it all in for ethereal "possibility?"

2. Does the author have any personal experience actually living with fear, or is he one of those Pollyannas who see the positive in everything and wouldn't know an external competitive threat or internal political maneuver if it hit him with a two-by-four?

Well, since you asked...

1. Yes, I see the upside of prudence and restraint.

2. Yes, I've lived with enough fear and anxiety to know what the experience is like.

The title of this book is a great description of my journey, and may be of yours as well. This is going to get personal fast, so stick with me or skip ahead if you must. When I was six, my parents got divorced. Like many kids in that situation, I learned to distrust the possibility of relationship and marriage. Only in the past ten years and through marriage to a wonderful woman have I warmed to the idea that relationships actually can work out. When I was seven, another boy my age got angry at me for excluding him from a game of kickball, so he jumped on my back, knocked me down, and held a knife to my throat for quite some time. I got away unscathed physically, but with a fear of knives and of being attacked that persists to this day. In seventh grade, I raised $150 by selling raffle tickets door to door in the hopes of winning the grand prize for selling the most tickets: a boom box. The evening before the competition ended, after it was too dark outside to sell any more, the most popular kid in the class called me up and casually asked me how many tickets I had sold. Not suspecting anything, I told him. The next day, he won the competition. It turns out that immediately after he called me, he sold his father the final 50 tickets—just enough to win.[2]

As an adult, I've been burned and knocked around as much as the next person. You know the experience of thinking you're part of the "in group" until one day a pivotal meeting takes place—and you're not invited—and the exclusion is obviously deliberate? Been there! You know what it's like to think that your organization is going to crush the competition until one day it gets blindsided by a mix of sharp maneuvers and malicious attacks? Been there, too!

Perhaps most importantly, my take on paranoia has been shaped by the many leaders I've had the privilege to coach and work with over the years. Although the negative stuff is only a portion of their experience, it is difficult to ignore. They've experienced all the political infighting, backstabbing, game-playing, and undermining you can imagine—as victim, as perpetrator, and sometimes as rescuer. You'll see some of those stories in the pages that follow.

Essentially, if you think the world is at least partly a scary place: I'm right there with you, my friend. That's why it's important for us to start this journey with a shared understanding that paranoia isn't all bad.

THE POSSIBILITY OF PARANOIA

The dictionary describes paranoia as "suspicion and mistrust of people or their actions without evidence or justification." Sound familiar? Perhaps you experienced it yesterday or last week or right before picking up this book. This basic combination of suspicion and mistrust pervades many organizations, not because human beings are bad, but instead because we are human. Everyone's brain contains parts inherited from earlier stages of evolution, like the instinctual ("reptilian") brain and the emotional brain.[3] Anything that triggers these earlier parts of the brain provokes a threat response that produces three possible reactions: fight, flee, or freeze. Gather enough human beings together and you get threat responses triggering other threat responses. Over time these threat responses get embedded in the culture and enshrined in control systems and other organizational policies. Thus, paranoid minds produce paranoid organizations.

This sounds gloomy—and we'll soon see that it is—but I start with the assumption that no instinct is 100 percent incorrect. Paranoia fits that bill. Although it is overrated as an organizing philosophy, it is underrated as a temporary mindset.

Recall the definition, "suspicion and mistrust of people or their actions without evidence or justification." What good is there in that? The same good that exists in any aspect of reality: it's what we have to work with, so we might as well make the best of it. To bury paranoia is to deny reality. Instead, let's ask ourselves: what's the possibility in paranoia?

In my mind, it's all about volume control. Paranoid thinking is like really loud music, the kind that pierces the eardrum. Your first instinct is to grab some earplugs, put your hands over your ears, or walk away. But sometimes excruciatingly loud music comes from a talented band whose music is over-amplified. Adjust the volume, and what was painful becomes pleasant to many and at least tolerable to all.

This is the possibility in paranoid thinking as it manifests in people and organizations. If you hear what sounds like paranoia, don't just believe it and don't just ignore it. Turn down the volume and listen for what's true or what's worth further investigation. For example:

- Your company's future is at risk because of missed opportunities, strategic miscalculations, or poor execution.
- Someone who reports to you wants your job.
- A competitor is trying to lure away your best talent.
- Several peers want the job you have your eyes on.
- A small group in your organization is breaking company rules and the law, which puts both the company and your credibility at risk.[4]
- Someone may stab you in the back and then deny to your face that they've done it.
- You have a leadership flaw that, if not resolved, could be fatal to your career.
- Your spouse is disappointed that you're never home and is considering leaving or cheating on you.

- Your unhealthy lifestyle makes you a strong candidate for a heart attack or stroke.

There's a lot of yuck in this muck. Some of that yuck is likely to happen. Now, you may wonder, what's the possibility hiding in that?

It's the same one provided by the rear-view camera on my car while it backs down the driveway. When the three-year-old kid who lives across the street runs away from his mother and into the path of my vehicle, I spot him on the camera and hit the brakes. Seeing disaster about to happen helps me prevent disaster.

This is the possibility of paranoia. This is the place where the ability to identify the brutal facts of the world meets the shining potential of the world you want to create. By naming the sharks swimming around you and the demons lurking within you, they no longer "have" you. You have them. This dramatically increases your degree of freedom in life. As you explore the tension between the world as it is and the world as you'd have it be, you create safe spaces for what Abraham Lincoln called "the better angels of our nature."

We need a new name for this aptitude. Let's call it *selective paranoia* and include it in our emotional tool kit. Selective paranoia means paying attention to the full range of present conditions and future scenarios, including those we might prefer to sweep under the rug. It is conscious, not reflexive. And it is worth remembering even as we consider the perils of paranoia.

Chapter 2

The Perils of Paranoia

ALTHOUGH PARANOIA MAY have promise as a short-term tactic, it doesn't fare so well as an ongoing leadership philosophy. Let's remember that paranoia means suspicion of people without justification. What's so wrong with building a culture and strategy around that?

Breaking the definition down, we see that:

paranoia = fear - rationale

In this equation, fear (the primary emotion of which suspicion is a variation) produces poor results, and the lack of rationale produces poor results. It logically follows that paranoia produces extremely poor results. Let's examine each part of the equation.

Fear: As a management approach, fear yields poor results. Research on leadership and employee engagement shows that:

- There is a strong correlation between employee engagement and productivity, customer engagement, quality, retention, safety, and profit. Studies by Gallup involving millions of employees around the world make this connection crystal clear.[5]

- Employees become dramatically less engaged when their bodies experience the threat ("fight, flight, or freeze") response. In the words of consultant David Rock, who uses brain research to rethink management practices, "because the [threat] response uses up oxygen and glucose from the blood, they are diverted from other parts of the brain, including the working memory function, which processes new information and ideas. This impairs analytic thinking, creative insight, and problem solving."[6]

- Triggering another person's threat response is not hard to do. All it takes is managing in a way that keeps employees from experiencing five social qualities: status, certainty, autonomy, relatedness, and fairness. Rock calls these the SCARF qualities. An employee whose status has been challenged or autonomy stripped away reacts the same way physiologically as if someone were pointing a gun at them. People who use paranoia to manage therefore have to try really hard to *not* trigger others' threat responses.

Rationale: This is an odd beast. In *making* decisions, it can be very useful—some managers won't leave home without it—but it isn't the only necessary aspect. The gut and the heart are equally important guides. But in *explaining* decisions to others, rationale is highly relevant. Remember that the C in the SCARF model stands for certainty. The brain craves it and, in its absence, plunges into the threat response. In the words of Rock, "Leaders and managers must thus work to create a perception of certainty to build confident and dedicated teams. Sharing business plans, rationales for change, and accurate maps of an organization's structure promotes this perception."

In summary, we see that when you take a negative (fear and its friend, mistrust) and subtract a positive (rationale), you get a very negative result. As a leadership philosophy, paranoia is bad news.

PARANOID CULTURE

If paranoid thinking is trouble, what about a paranoid culture?

Unfortunately, the bad news gets worse. In paranoid cultures, it's not just individual leaders and their teams who experience fear and distrust without rationale. The entire system—from written policies and incentives to unwritten codes of behavior—enforces paranoia and crowds out possibility. Bold new strategies fall short of their potential because, as Peter Drucker taught us, "culture eats strategy for breakfast."

Organizational culture is a huge topic. Instead of summarizing it, I'll illustrate it by looking at three expressions of paranoid culture that I've personally encountered: managing performance through forced ranking, requiring employee face time, and overscheduling.

Managing Performance Through Forced Ranking

A classic expression of paranoid culture is employee performance management, particularly the type that ranks people against each other. GE has used such a system for years and done quite well as a company. However, it's not clear whether their success is because or in spite of forced ranking. If you work at GE, your manager places you in one of three categories: high performer (the top 20%), middle performer (the middle 70%), or low performer (the bottom 10%). If you're a low performer, you get removed or improved. Sounds like meritocracy at its best, right? Not really. As USC management professor, John Boudreau, points out:

Is removing or improving the bottom 10 percent valuable in all cases? Certainly in some situations even the bottom 10 percent are doing an adequate job and are doing better than those who could be hired or promoted. By definition, continually removing or improving the bottom 10 percent will make the bottom 10 percent more similar to the middle 70 percent and thus make removing the bottom 10 percent less effective in improving workforce quality.[7]

What about companies that rank employees but don't automatically remove people? A clue may come from Microsoft. After years of extraordinary success, the company stumbled during the decade after the year 2000. A cover story in the August 2012 issue of *Vanity Fair* explores why. The author, Kurt Eichenwald, reveals a startling discovery:

Every current and former Microsoft employee I interviewed— *every one*—cited stack ranking as the most destructive process inside of Microsoft...

"The behavior this engenders, people do everything they can to stay out of the bottom bucket," one Microsoft engineer said. "People responsible for features will openly sabotage other people's efforts. One of the most valuable things I learned was to give the appearance of being courteous while withholding just enough information from colleagues to ensure they didn't get ahead of me on the rankings."

Worse, because the reviews came every six months, employees and their supervisors—who were also ranked—focused on their short-term performance, rather than on longer efforts to innovate.

"The six-month reviews forced a lot of bad decision-making," one software designer said. "People planned their days and their years around the review, rather than around products. You really had to focus on the six-month performance, rather than on doing what was right for the company."[8]

Like many artifacts of a paranoid culture, ranking systems also waste extraordinary amounts of time. As a manager you spend time proposing rank orders and debating them with others. You spend time worrying about how you're going to explain to a perfectly competent employee that they are below average. You spend time meeting with employees. And you spend more time in subsequent weeks and months dealing with the emotional fallout.

How about everyone else? The biggest time sink here is the effort it takes to position yourself with your boss, your boss's boss, and your boss's boss's peers. Looking good gets rewarded more than doing what's good for the company. Any new idea that challenges others' perspective or status also threatens your own compensation and job security.

In companies that employ such a system—and I've worked with several—many people spend performance review month in a mood of resignation. They go to all the same meetings and have all the same conversations, but with a bit less energy and a lot less enthusiasm. It's not that they cannot tolerate the system or don't know how to navigate through it. Instead, it's that they despise and resent it even while believing there is nothing they can do about it.

This is a bummer to witness, so I keep looking for the right person to whom I can humbly suggest, "Toss the whole thing out already, will you?" Audacious? For sure. But no more audacious than supporting a friend in quitting smoking or taking the car keys out of the hands of an intoxicated party guest.

Wouldn't it be cool to see how much positive energy gets freed—and how much time is created—by an organization taking this single bold act?

Requiring Face Time

Telecommuting is apparently the wave of the future. Employees can work from home, save on gas, and have greater flexibility. A significant amount of research supports the business value of honoring employee autonomy and trusting their intrinsic motivation. (For examples, see *Drive* by Daniel Pink.)[9] But telecommuting exists far more in principle than in practice, particularly in paranoid cultures. What's the situation in your organization? I expect it falls into one of three categories: (1) it prohibits telecommuting; (2) the formal policy allows it, and the culture supports it; or (3) the formal policy allows it, but the culture discourages it.

Why do managers discourage telecommuting? Because they were taught that "if I see you, I know you're getting things done. If I can't see you, then there's no way to know." This assumption flies in the face of all that we know about people's intrinsic motivation to work: the business value from the 98 percent of honest employees trumps the risk from the 2 percent who would game the system.[10] But that's rational thinking, and the belief about face time exists in the realm of myth. Paranoid? For sure. But also pervasive.

What about employees? Why might they avoid telecommuting? The root is similar: fear. The fear of being punished by their manager. The fear of missing something important.

Now, not all of these fears are unfounded. As we've seen, many times they are worth considering. But in paranoid cultures, people's fear and distrust exist without rationale.

What's lost is the possibility of having a more flexible work life and all the benefits it can bring.

Wouldn't it be nice to find a way to support employees in choosing when and where to work? Wouldn't it be great to give them a chance to show that the gains in productivity, engagement, and morale by the many far outweigh the abuses by the few?

Overscheduling

The days of back-to-back meetings have ended. Managers now live in an era of back-to-back-to-back-to-back meetings—and that's on a light day! If you had to custom design a schedule that would shrink people's moods and suck out their energy, you couldn't design one better than the back-to-back-to-back-to-back. In fact, research shows that high performers in every field do exactly the opposite. They go through a perform-renew-perform-renew cycle that gives them a break every 90 minutes.[11] But this does not occur in most organizations, and certainly not in paranoid cultures.

Now, you might think that all these meetings are a good idea. Rather than sitting at their desks, managers are out talking with employees and each other. They're getting things done together, rather than alone. Isn't that what collaboration is all about?

I once asked this to an executive I was coaching. His response: "Hell no!"

Managers waste enormous amounts of time in meetings. You know this. You've complained about it. Everyone you know has complained about it. I want to convince you that it doesn't have to be that way—and, as I'll discuss in the chapter "Managing Commitments," that there are practical steps you can take to free yourself from meeting-overload.

But first, I'd like to describe the managerial habits that cause overscheduling:

- *Scheduling meetings that don't have to happen.* This includes everything from work groups and task forces that lack a clear purpose to standing meetings that have lost their rationale for being.

- *Scheduling meetings for more time than you need.* Parkinson's Law says that "work expands so as to fill the time available for its completion." The longer you schedule a meeting, the more time you'll spend in that meeting.

- *Wasting time in the meetings you do attend.* Have you ever calculated the percentage of meeting time that adds value (productive conversations about important topics) versus the percentage that is wasteful (unfocused conversations, tangential topics, and unnecessary conflict)? Waste consumes a big piece of the pie.

- *Assuming you need to be at every meeting.* "If I don't go, I may miss something important." Or so you think. Have you ever actually calculated the cost of missing something? Simply multiply the cost of the missed experience by the probability of that experience occurring in your absence. Now compare that to the opportunity cost of *not* accomplishing something else instead of attending that meeting. Which cost is larger?

- *Being physically present—and absent in every other way.* Because you are afraid of missing something, you go to a meeting. But because you really don't need to be there and have other things to do, you work on your laptop most of the time. You might even send an email to the person sitting next to you in the meeting working on her laptop. If all goes well, she'll whisper back to you, "Thanks for the email. You saved my butt on that one."

- *Assuming other managers need to be at meetings you have called.* There is great value in ensuring that conversations reflect a wide range of perspectives. Excluding people for the sake of excluding them is a lousy practice. That's not what we're talking about here. My point is that you may be inviting more people to meetings than are needed, either to add value or to ensure a feeling of inclusion. Said differently, when other managers attend your meetings when their time would produce greater value elsewhere, you own part of the responsibility for their wasted time.

WHY DO WE PUT UP WITH PARANOID CULTURES?

If paranoid leadership and paranoid cultures are such losing propositions, why are they so prevalent? As we've seen, they are often a natural result of having large numbers of reptilian brains colliding in small spaces, not knowing any other way to be together. Biology feeds habit, and habit shapes destiny. From this history is born.

Let's morph the question a bit. Why have a number of highly respected senior executives spoken out in favor of paranoid leadership over the years? The answer is different for each individual, but in the case of one prominent CEO, it turns out that the book should not be judged by its cover.

CHAPTER 3

WHAT ANDY GROVE KNEW

"HOW A COMPANY handles the process of getting through [difficult times] depends on a very 'soft' almost touchy-feely issue: how management reacts emotionally to the crisis."[12]
—Andy Grove

Intel Corporation's largest site of operations in the world is 20 miles from my home. Its most famous and admired CEO, Andy Grove, wrote a book about leadership, *Only the Paranoid Survive*, which looks like a straight-up argument for paranoid thinking. But, is it?

I don't think so. Once you read beyond the cover, the book provides a far more complex, nuanced, and mature view of leadership than the title suggests. For Grove, strategic inflection points (events that change the way we think and act) offer promises as well as threats. (Paranoid people see everything as a threat.) Middle managers, particularly "Cassandras" at the "periphery," often see these inflection points first, so

Grove suggests that executives should "hear them out, learn what they know and understand why it affects them the way it does."[13] This requires openness, which is the antithesis of paranoia. Better yet, he encourages executives to create an environment of rigorous debate, which "is only possible when people can speak their minds without fear of punishment."[14] This isn't a given because, as Grove states, "It takes many years of consistent conduct to eliminate fear of punishment as an inhibitor of strategic discussion [but] only one incident to introduce it."[15] In other words, to paraphrase FDR, the main thing to fear is fear itself.

These passages—and the book as a whole—suggest to me that the piece of writing most associated with Andy Grove's brand of leadership is far from an argument for paranoia. Instead, it's a powerful case for alert and curious leaders who are humble enough to know what they don't know and courageous enough to listen to middle managers' heresies without branding them as heretics.

So when I speak below about the *perils of paranoia*, I am not critiquing Grove's book. In fact, as we shall see, true paranoia gets in the way of what Grove expounds in his book. True paranoia:

- Makes it difficult to differentiate the true strategic inflection points from all the other potential threats because the paranoid mind does not think clearly!

- Inhibits middle managers from speaking candidly to senior executives out of fear of punishment.

- Deters senior executives from listening to middle managers' most provocative perspectives out of fear of being embarrassed, looking weak, or looking indecisive.

Grove may or may not have been a paranoid person. And I'll leave it up to those who worked with him at Intel to assess whether or not he built a paranoid culture. But one thing is clear to me: his book is not an endorsement of paranoia. On the contrary, it advocates for several practices that I associate with *possibility leadership*. A more accurate (if less marketable) title would have been *Only the Alert and Humble Survive* or *Only Those Who Listen to the Paranoid Survive*.

CHAPTER 4

POSSIBILITY LEADERSHIP

SO IF PARANOIA as management philosophy is a lemon, what makes us believe that possibility thinking is lemonade?

It helps to broaden the last part of the question. Thinking is just part of leadership. There is also sensing, feeling, interpreting, and seeing—not to mention speaking and listening! So let's not set our sights on possibility thinking alone. Let's aim higher, for *possibility leadership*.

Possibility leadership is not the opposite of paranoid leadership; you can't develop it by simply acting less paranoid. It's an entirely different beast. And it arises by focusing not on the results you produce, but on *how* you produce results. This *how* includes a number of actions that are visible to others, which I call the *outer practices* of possibility leadership:

- Hold *conversations for possibility* where *what if* trumps *what could go wrong*.

- Build trust in moment-to-moment interactions by *turning toward* other people rather than away from or against them.

- Channel negative energy into positive energy by *flipping complaints into commitments.*

- Evoke possibility amidst disagreement by *arguing better* and *neutralizing enemies* (which is neither as diabolical nor as simple as it sounds).

- Help people see themselves as protagonists in a positive future by *telling stories.*

- Develop the single competence that underlies all of the others— *listening like a master.*

- Generate better stuff to listen to by *asking great questions.*

These outer practices hold great potential for helping you grow as a leader and as a person. There is a lot to learn about them, and you could spend a lifetime learning these things. However, I think you'll find it easier to get traction as you take on any given outer practice, when you simultaneously take on at least one *inner practice* of possibility leadership. These inner practices complement the outer practices in the way that exercise complements nutrition in losing weight. So I encourage you to consider these inner practices:

- *Visualize* a future you desire.

- Discover organizational strategies and discern human strengths by *seeing patterns.*

- Focus like a laser beam on your greatest weakness by *healing your Achilles heel.*

- Catch yourself in delusions of grandeur by *calling B.S. on yourself.*

- Get all of this done without adding to your stress by *managing commitments.*

- Imitate high performers in other fields by *managing your physical energy.*

- Ensure that you are well positioned for possibility leadership by *posturing* (which is more physical and less political than it sounds).

Chapter 5

Start with Purpose

AT THIS POINT, let's assume you're excited about possibility leadership and ready to learn about ways of practicing it. Before we embark on this journey, I invite you to consider a question: *for the sake of what* do you want to practice possibility leadership? In other words, what is the purpose behind your leadership?

I ask this question for both philosophical and practical reasons. Philosophically, if leaders are going to get better at leading, I prefer that they do so to achieve something larger than themselves, to promote the greater good. Practically, having a sense of purpose makes it dramatically more likely that you will both start and persevere in practicing possibility leadership.

The practices I describe will challenge you and support you in becoming a better version of yourself. This involves ending old habits and starting new ones and, in turn, stepping into parts of yourself that you have intuited, but never fully trusted. As a new version of yourself is born, an older version gradually dies or at least shrinks in importance. As you read these words, you may be feeling excitement, fear, or both. One thing I can guarantee is that taking on new practices will be messy, uncomfortable, and confusing.

So why bother?

Seriously, why bother investing all the energy to make a shift in yourself? Why bother taking the risk of speaking and listening in new ways, of mending troubled relationships, of improving your posture and physical energy?

In my experience, one key factor differentiates managers who carry this hard work to completion from others who barely get out of the starting blocks: a sense of purpose beyond their own narrow self-interest. Getting a raise or promotion is great, but neither provides enough fuel to sustain the practice of possibility leadership. The source of such fuel is what the French call a *raison d'etre*, or reason for being: something you are trying to create, renew, rejuvenate, or replenish. This could be bringing to market a marvelous new technology, like a scalable substitute for fossil fuels. It could be teaching young women in the developing world to read. Or it could be building an organization where people feel safe and "at home."

Without such a purpose, everything I'm going to suggest in this book will feel like drudgery—at best! With such a purpose, the hard work of practicing possibility leadership feels like a smart investment, one with risks, of course, but also the possibility of a positive return.

Discovering your sense of purpose isn't the easiest thing in the world to do. You may choose to avoid the question entirely, and for good reason: inquiring into your purpose makes you aware of how out of alignment your actions are with it. Conversely, if you don't know your purpose, there is little risk of feeling shame at being out of alignment with it! Contrary to myth, ostriches don't actually bury their heads in the sand. (Although they do lower their beaks down there several times a day to turn their eggs.) When predators show up, they run away. Why shouldn't managers do the same?

Zoological humor aside, what's it like to ask yourself about your purpose? If this exploration is uncomfortable but not treacherous, I encourage you to continue it by asking yourself a few questions:

- What do you want to be known for?

- What are your unique strengths and how do they intersect with what your organization, community, or world need right now?

- What do you feel passionate about taking a stand on?

- What does the world want from you?

- What would you risk embarrassment or fear to bring into being?

- Who would you be if you weren't held back by the past, but instead were pulled by the future?

As you explore these questions, you may notice that your purpose is not one thing but many things, and these many things are not always consistent. You may also find that there are actually levels of purpose within you, some more inclusive than others. I encourage you to call out these differences by sorting your potential purposes into a set of descriptive categories. In particular, start by naming the purposes that involve standing up for yourself and then expand outward from there.

This notion of expanding outward is captured by the concept of moral development. Psychologist Lawrence Kohlberg named the stages of moral development; his colleague Carol Gilligan updated them to accurately measure women, whose morality grows through "ethics of care" rather than "ethics of justice."[16] Ken Wilber renamed the stages "spans of moral concern" or simply "moral spans." Whatever terminology you use, the idea is that the wider your moral span, the greater the number of people and interests you consider when making decisions.

To distinguish your purposes, I suggest placing each potential purpose in one of the following categories. Each category represents a distinct moral span and carries specific implications for your leadership:

Me Leadership: You work and practice for the sake of your own achievement, happiness, health, and well being. Your concern is yourself and everything needed to keep you safe, secure, and content. This level of purpose may seem less noble than the two levels that follow, but it's not. In fact, it is foundational both practically and developmentally. On a practical level, if you can't define what's good for you, what business do you have advocating for what's good for others? From a developmental perspective, researchers tell us that humans need to develop a healthy egocentrism (*Me*) before it is possible to foster a healthy ethnocentrism (*Us*) or world-centrism (*All of Us*). This is why toddlers don't actually understand the meaning of sharing, teenagers struggle with fitting in, and most adults don't truly identify with a purpose beyond their family or organization until they are in their 40s and 50s.

Us Leadership: Your purpose—indeed, your entire sense of self—expands to include your team, your organization, your family, your tribe, your country, and so on. This is a major step forward. It means you exist for something larger than yourself. This is not better or worse than Me Leadership, just more inclusive. And it comes in both healthy forms (rooting for your favorite sports team, celebrating your religion's holidays, eating Thanksgiving dinner with your family) and unhealthy forms (picking a fight with the soccer referee who gives your daughter a yellow card, denouncing people of other faiths, and killing turkeys for the sport of it rather than to eat).

All of Us Leadership: In *The Needs of Strangers*, Canadian writer Michael Ignatieff asks, "What do we owe strangers?" It's a fascinating question because everything in our lives is touched by people we will never see or know. If you were to care as much about all people, including those who don't look or sound or live like you, as you care about yourself or those who are more similar to you, what would the expression of that care be? In asking this, I want to distinguish outer actions from inner purposes. When I was 18 years old, I participated in a Take Back the Night March on my university's campus. This looked noble and was, at least in the sense that the purpose was to declare the rights of women to feel safe after dark. But if you had excavated my mind, you would have found that I participated mostly to feel good about myself, distinguish myself from other men, and possibly even attract a woman from down the hall whom I fancied and who invited me to participate. From where I sit today, I would call that a clear Me motivation. So, as you start to distinguish different levels of purpose for yourself, please be mindful of All of Us appearances masking Me intentions. There is nothing to be ashamed of. We all do it. But be honest and put these purposes into the Me Leadership category.

I hope you find this exercise to be illuminating. I have. Working through it brought me to my current purpose: to develop great leaders in clean technology and sustainability. Currently, such leaders represent less than 10 percent of my clientele. This could be a reason to feel embarrassed. Or it could be a reason to feel energized, have more conversations, and build relationships with new organizations. Which interpretation do you recommend I choose?

And, while we are on the topic, what is your purpose?

CHAPTER 6

FOCUS ON ONE THING

IN THE NEXT two sections, you will learn about 15 practices—eight outer and seven inner—of possibility leadership. I encourage you to think of these as being on a menu, not an agenda. Your success as a leader and your happiness as a person don't depend on doing all 15 practices. In fact, if you try to do all 15, expect disappointment, if not distress.

My advice is to pick two practices—one outer and one inner—and give them your full attention. Here's why:

- Focusing your attention will give you better results than dispersing it widely.

- Selecting the highest leverage practices will give you benefits across many domains of your life. This assumes that you deliberately practice them, which is the subject of Part Four.

Despite this advice, you may find yourself so excited by the range of practices that you want to take up many of them. On the other hand, you may feel so overwhelmed by the amount of "work" that you feel like throwing the whole thing out. In either case, keep your mind tuned into this question: *What's the one thing that has the greatest potential to improve your leadership?*

Pick it. Practice it.

Practice it some more.

PART TWO

THE OUTER PRACTICES

Chapter 7

Holding Conversations for Possibility

"AS I STARTED [in 1985] to discuss the possibility of getting out of the memory chip business with some of my associates, I had a hard time getting the words out of my mouth without equivocation. It was just too difficult a thing to say."[17]

—Andy Grove

An amazing amount of work happens through conversation. Name any significant thing you've done in your life, and I bet you couldn't have done it without talking with someone about something. Right?

Yet we have this bizarre distinction between "talk" and "action." It's really an unfortunate use of words. I prefer to speak about different kinds of talk, some more action-oriented than others. One type of talk, *conversation for possibility*, is a crucial practice for possibility leadership. At heart this is extraordinarily simple: have a "what if" conversation about the future. Pick something that you and others might enjoy doing and discuss what it would be like, how it might look, sound, and feel, and what benefits might come from the experience. Don't ask what could go wrong. Ask what could go right. Don't get hooked on how somebody tried it in the past. Focus on how you might do it in the future. Most importantly, listen for what is possible, and if you don't hear anything, ask others if they do.

A PERSONAL EXPERIENCE

To give you a richer sense of conversations for possibility, this is the story of how I first learned about them:

Thirteen years ago in the lobby of a hotel in San Francisco's Union Square, a senior manager at HP was coaching me on how to get a girlfriend. I had just moved across the country from Michigan and was trying to make a few life changes. One was to get into a good relationship. My coach and I sat across a small round table, and I told her the story of my dating life: what I was looking for, how I approached things, who I had been dating, and how things tended to turn out. The full story, which I had never told anyone before, took two hours. She listened attentively the entire time. When I was done, my coach asked, "So, Amiel, I can see how important a relationship is to you and all the effort you've put into dating. What do you think is getting in the way?"

"I, um, really don't know."

"Let me give you my take." She drew a picture of three concentric circles—labeled, from the inside out, *Relationship*, *Possibility*, and *Action*. "There are three types of conversations. Each one has a purpose and is important in dating and the rest of life. A conversation for relationship is about exploring interests, finding out what the other person likes and doesn't like, so you have a sense of whether this is someone you'd want to spend more time with. A conversation for possibility is about *what if*. You pick something that interests both of you and talk about what it would be like to do that—say, visiting the zoo, hiking in the forest, or going to a concert. A conversation for action is where you actually invite her out onto a date—it's the first time you actually make a request or offer."

"OK," I said. "That makes sense. What's the problem?"

"I think you're jumping too quickly into conversations for action and skipping over the other two types of conversation. As a result, you're asking women out before you've gotten to know them and before they've gotten to know you."

In other words, bold action is great, but not without discernment. Conversations for action are necessary, but may fall flat without the presence of relationship and a sense of possibility.

Although I hated to admit it, she had a point. Once I found a woman attractive, I tended to plunge right in and ask her out. This led to one of two things happening. Either she said "no," and I felt disappointed. Or she said "yes," and I ended up going out with someone who was pretty, but not particularly interesting to be with. Either scenario made a sustained relationship unlikely.

My coach's insights were so on the mark that I decided to heed Buckminster Fuller's saying that if you don't act on a new idea in the first 15 minutes, it will never happen. That evening, at a party, I made a point while talking with women to listen for shared interests rather than just following the call of attraction. In a couple cases, I found myself bored or at least not enthused and excused myself. In one case, when I observed a great deal of common interests, I switched into a conversation for possibility. The details escape my memory, but it was something like, "So, I just had this image of us going out for sushi. Humor me for a minute: if we did that, what do you imagine you'd order?" I'm sure I was awkward—beginners always are—but it was a first attempt at exploring possibility before going into action. I ended up asking her out.[18]

In subsequent weeks and months, I made a point of paying attention to what kind of conversation I was having—not only in dating, but in all domains of life. I watched for two things:

- How much time I was spending in each type of conversation. Was I overdoing it on conversations for action? Or, in my quest to practice, did the pendulum swing too far toward conversations for relationship or possibility?

- How well I was sequencing the conversations. Did I first use relationship, then possibility, then action?

Over time, I found that I got better and better at this. My competence at conversation increased from mediocre to adequate. And it showed. I started enjoying the experience of dating more and found a greater sense of flow in work and friendships. Life was not perfect by any means, but it was the beginning of an important journey.

CONVERSATIONS FOR POSSIBILITY IN ORGANIZATIONS

After several years of practicing this myself, I began to introduce it to my organizational clients. In one case, a colleague and I led the senior management team of a large startup factory through an unusual exercise. We had people seated at tables of six. Our assignment for each group was to have a conversation about where to have lunch. There was a catch: two people were supposed to talk about what mattered to them in picking a restaurant (ambience, type of food, service, etc); two were told to describe what it would be like to go to one particular restaurant they liked; and the other two were instructed to propose specific places at specific times.

The intent of the exercise was to see how groups experienced having three very different types of conversations at the same time. The consistent result was confusion and frustration. One person would ask, "How about we meet at Joe's Bar and Grill at 12:30?" Another would answer, "I'm really looking for a place that will get us in and out quickly."

And the third would say, "What if we were to find a place with an outdoor patio?" Three completely different conversations!

The amazing part wasn't that there was so much confusion and misunderstanding, but that it was so familiar to everyone. This bizarre way of talking around each other (without anyone naming it as such) operated much of the time, and it was costing them time and energy. In addition, in the push for fast decisions, the conversations for relationship and possibility typically got the short end of the stick, so the people initiating them gave up and went along with the pure action orientation.

What alternative did we introduce to this group? The very practice I suggest for you: start having more conversations for possibility. When you do, make sure that they are about topics that interest all participants. This requires knowing what people care about, which, in turn, depends upon astute observation coupled with prior conversations for relationship.

In other words, if you want to have better action and more trust, start by having conversations for relationship and possibility. This is so simple, but if your organizational culture has never encouraged it, it may not come easily to you.

More and Better Conversations for Relationship

My advice for having better conversations for relationship is to keep things very simple. Start by doing them one-on-one over coffee or lunch—or spontaneously when you can grab someone for a few minutes. An ideal length of time is 30-60 minutes, but sometimes 5-10 minutes will do just fine.

If having one-on-one meetings is part of your organization's culture, great. If not, this may feel a bit riskier to you, so frame the invitation like this, "I'm working on X project and know you're working on Y. I think we may be able to help each other and I'd like to have a two-way chat to explore where our interests may overlap. Would you be up for a 30-minute coffee in the next few weeks?"

Now here are a few tips for having the conversation itself:

1. *Start briefly with context.* "Thanks for agreeing to meet. I'd like to ask you some questions about Y and would be happy to talk about X. Let's see where our interests overlap."

2. *Ask a few simple, open-ended questions:*
   - Can you tell me more about Y?
   - What are you hoping to achieve?
   - How are things looking right now?

3. *Listen very specifically for what the other person cares about.* Make a note of it in your mind—or include it in your meeting notes.

4. *Ask follow-up questions:*
   - What makes that important to you?
   - What was that like for you?
   - What do you like most about____?
   - What do you like least about____?
   - Could you say more about that?
   - Could you help me understand what you meant when you said____?

5. *Briefly summarize* the interests you have heard and ask, "Have I heard you correctly?"

6. *Be prepared to talk* about what you're working on and what makes it important to you. This is a good time to be real and err on the side of disclosing more than you ordinarily might.

When I ask leaders to hold conversations for relationship, the typical response I hear afterward is, "I got a much better understanding of where she's coming from than I ever have before."

This, of course, is the point: to get to know others' perspectives and interests so we can consider what possibilities we might explore with them.

More and Better Conversations for Possibility

That brings us to the main focus of this chapter: how to have more and better conversations for possibility.

The quantity of such conversations depends upon three main factors:

1. *Your mood.* If you're moping around in a mood of resignation or stomping around in a mood of resentment, your orientation will be to avoid conversations for possibility. It won't occur to you to initiate them and if others do, you'll steer clear.

2. *Your understanding of what others care about.* How well do you understand the interests and concerns of the people you work with? The more you know, the more ideas you'll have for conversations for possibility.

3. *Your willingness to show up.*

Once you agree to show up, you can increase the odds of the conversation being of high quality by doing the following:

1. *Pick a topic that involves shared interests* of the people involved or invite people who share an interest. It has to be something everyone cares about—not equally, but at least above a certain threshold of concern.

2. *Call it a "conversation for possibility."* This is not a time to be fuzzy. As we saw with the lunch decision exercise, weird things happen when people don't know what kind of conversation they are in.

3.   *Remind everyone of the ground rules.* Do talk about the future, do talk about the good that can come, and do piggyback on others' ideas. Don't offer critiques (save these for later).

4.   *Close the laptops* to avoid distractions. Use a white board or sticky notes to track ideas.

5.   *Create a "parking lot"* for requests, offers, and anything that is outside of the conversation for possibility, including tough questions and critiques. Often the best parking lot is the one you maintain yourself. For example, if you're in the discussion and you have an idea that doesn't fit the ground rules, write it down. I know this sounds heretical, but you really don't have to say everything you think the moment it enters your mind. What you need is a trusted place to put it so you have confidence it will reenter your view later.

6.   *Say "Wouldn't it be nice if..."* This phrase is a great way to introduce a possibility without advocating for it or making a commitment to it.

As I said, the hardest part of this may be getting started, simply because it's so unusual in your organization's culture. Once you get the ideas and imaginations flowing, you may be surprised what positive results ensue with relatively little effort. It may not look pretty or go flawlessly. The group will get off topic. People's critical minds will intervene. Someone's laptop will spontaneously open, and their fingers will mysteriously start typing. But this is all part of learning something new together, of building a new collective habit.

CHAPTER 8

TURNING TOWARD OTHERS

"THE BASIC PRINCIPLE that regulates how relationships work and also determines a great deal about how conflict between people can be regulated…has to do with the way people, in mundane moments in everyday life, make attempts at emotional communication, and how others around them respond, or fail to respond, to these attempts."[19]

—John Gottman, *The Relationship Cure*

A conversation for possibility creates a safe space for possibility thinking. That's great, but what about the fifty other conversations you have? How do you create space for possibility leadership there?

One way is to pay attention to *how* you interact with others no matter what you are talking about. Every day you have dozens of conversations ranging in length from a 30-second chat in the hall to a 2-hour meeting. Each conversation includes a multitude of subtle back-and-forth exchanges between you and others. The relational quality of these exchanges—how specifically you choose to respond to each other—has a substantial impact on your emotions and those of others. I refer to such exchanges as *micro-interactions*. They happen so quickly and habitually that you often don't notice them and can't describe them afterwards if asked. Yet, on emotional and gut levels, micro-interactions register in a big way.

Have you ever noticed that some people give you positive vibes when you are around them even when you are disagreeing vehemently, whereas others consistently rub you the wrong way even on seemingly uncontroversial topics? As I'll discuss later, this discrepancy may reflect your listening filter, the specific way you interpret your experiences. Or, if it turns out that many others experience similar reactions to these two individuals, the difference may be in the two of them more than in you.

To understand this difference in a way that allows you to bring a mood of possibility into your micro-interactions, let's turn to John Gottman, Emeritus Professor of Psychology at the University of Washington. Gottman earned fame as the person who can watch a newlywed couple interact briefly behind a one-way mirror and then predict with 90 percent accuracy whether they will still be married in five years. His predictions are based on very careful observation of the micro-interactions that happen between couples when discussing everyday topics. He has found that a small set of behaviors, like showing contempt toward your partner or withdrawing from connection, are highly correlated with divorce, whereas other behaviors, like gently supporting each other, are correlated with a stable marriage.

If this sounds obvious to you—*be nice, don't be mean*—I agree. The real value in Gottman's work, and the one that applies equally well to leadership, is that he distinguishes three ways you can *turn* when somebody else reaches out to you within a conversation. Gottman calls this reaching out a "bid for connection." Bids can be large ("Would you like this job?") or small ("Can you hand me the marker?"), subtle ("I was impressed with that speech") or direct ("I want you to give that speech at all seven sites"). In all of these cases, Gottman's research suggests that the person receiving the bid has three choices for responding: turn toward the other person, turn away from them, or turn against them.

Consider this simple example: You're walking in the parking lot before work and bump into a former colleague. The two of you worked closely on a project until she left for another team. You tell her that the old team is getting together over lunch in two weeks to celebrate the success of the project and "it would be great if you could make it." You've made a bid for connection. Your colleague can respond in one of three ways:

- She can *turn toward* you. "Yes, that sounds great, I'm there. Thanks for inviting me." But what if she cannot make it? She can still turn toward you by saying, "Bummer, I'll be out of the country then, but otherwise I'd love to come. Is there any flexibility in the date? If not, can I join you all some other time?"

- She can *turn away* from you by ignoring you ("Sorry, gotta run"), changing the topic without acknowledging your question ("Whatever happened to Smithy?"), or physically turning her body in a different direction.

- She can *turn against* you. The cold approach: "Nope, I've moved on. Not interested." The critical approach: "So, you guys actually made it. I never would have expected that given the caliber of the team." Or a tone of contempt: "Are you serious? Don't you remember *anything* of what things were like?"

One bid for connection. Three very different responses. As you imagine yourself on the receiving end of each response, what is your experience like? How does it feel to be with this person? Are you more or less likely to make a future bid for connection with her?

Gottman found that the three responses have dramatically different effects on relationships. Turning toward produces more bidding and responding and causes relationships to grow. Turning away and turning against both reduce the amount of future bidding. But whereas turning away increases conflict by producing hurt feelings and causes relationships to end relatively quickly, turning against leads to conflict-avoidance by suppressing feelings and causes relationships to end more slowly.[20]

Gottman's research team also found that when one person makes repeated bids for connection and the other consistently turns away from or against them—which he calls "unrequited turning"—the relationship heads south quickly:

> "Once bidders are ignored or rejected, they usually give up trying to connect in the same way again...People seem to lose heart...Among people in stable marriages, spouses re-bid just 20 percent of the time. In marriages that are headed for divorce, people hardly re-bid at all. Instead they simple fade away from conversations, relinquishing their attempts to connect."

Do these research findings sound familiar to you? They sure match my experience, both professionally and personally. Several examples come to mind:

- Several years ago, I had the opportunity to see in action an executive who was expert at turning toward others. He is known in his company as one of its most promising leaders, someone who could run a Fortune 500 company in the next decade. On the one hand, he does many of the things other hard-nosed leaders in his company do—set high expectations, hold people accountable, and ask challenging questions. On the other hand, he does these things in a way that others enjoy being around him. He has this effect because he consistently turns toward others even while disagreeing with them. I once heard a conversation in which he was angry and willing to show it, yet there was still the sense that he was turning toward people involved in the situation. This is not easy to do! Consequently, even in the midst of strong disagreement, the collective mood around him was positive.

- Not long ago I coached a different executive who was a pro at turning against others' bids for connection. No matter what others would say, he would respond with some version of "No." Sometimes it was a gentle, "No, that's not going to work." Sometimes it was a more hard-edged criticism or insult. Even when he liked what the other person was saying, he would start out by pointing out where he disagreed. I remember talking with him once after a meeting where I had observed this happen literally thirty times with the same person, whose energy level had dropped more and more with each iteration. I said to my client, "You sure did turn against her a lot." His response: "No, actually I really respect her a lot. I just want to make sure she is thinking things through. There's so much that can go wrong." Turning against others' bids can become so habitual that it affects every exchange. It took quite a bit of practice, reflection, and feedback for this executive to shift his responses to everyday situations.

- I have an acquaintance who is extraordinarily gifted at turning away from people. No matter what you say to him, he ignores you, changes the topic, or simply stares off into the abyss. He has a successful career and by most measures is a mature adult, yet in the most routine interactions about the most basic things, he cannot help but turn away. I've offered feedback and even described the impact on me, but I've come to the conclusion it's a lost cause. Why do I share this example? Because if possibility leadership includes the practice of turning toward others, it also includes the practice of not getting entangled in continuing to bid for connection with people who cannot or will not turn toward you. As we'll see in the chapter on "neutralizing enemies," it may still be useful to develop a neutral and respectful relationship with this person, but not to extend yourself beyond the response you are receiving.

- I'm currently involved in a project with a small team of people who are skilled both individually and as a team at turning toward. It's not that they do anything big or momentous. It's more how they respond to all the little things that comprise a project: asking for information via email, requesting a reschedule for a meeting, talking about a draft report, appreciating hard work, passing a napkin across the table at lunch, and so on. I have a sense, even when we see things very differently, that they trust and respect me. This is not something I imagine or remember from four years ago, but it's something that now gets renewed and reinforced with each micro-interaction.

This "turning" stuff is a big deal, and it comes down to an extremely simple idea: the way you respond in a microsecond to another person's bid for connection, when multiplied over hundreds of interactions, constitutes your relationship with them. It *is* your relationship with them.

Try on this concept for a moment, and I think you'll find that the implications are momentous. If you want to build an organization of people who are highly engaged and filled with a mood of possibility, one of the most effective things you can do is to start turning toward people—not just once, but continuously as a regular practice. Consider that in an average 60-minute meeting, you have anywhere from 5 to 50 opportunities to turn toward others. How many of these opportunities will you seize? In the same meeting you have a similar number of temptations to turn away from or against others. How many of these will you succumb to?

The bad news is that this takes effort. You can't just interact with people. You have to observe yourself interacting with them.

The good news is that the slightest shift, when repeated hundreds of times, can elevate your leadership substantially. Attend to the small stuff, over and over again, and you'll produce some really positive big stuff.

CHAPTER 9

FLIPPING COMPLAINTS TO

COMMITMENTS

"BEHIND EVERY COMPLAINT is an idea or belief or a value that a person is committed to. Otherwise why be upset? A person who complains that his boss is a jerk might be committed to the idea of having a relationship with a boss that is based on respect and trust."[21]

—Lisa Lahey, co-author, *Immunity to Change*

I'm big into flipping things. Burgers, eggs, omelets—and words. (Notice I didn't say "middle fingers"—that's in the other guy's book.) Flipping words means more than just saying something different. It's a literal substitution. You take something you are about to say and replace it with something else because the new words reflect the better version of you.

This happened to me in a powerful way when I was in my late 20s. One day over lunch a friend pointed out to me how often I used the words *should* and *need to*. This was less a criticism than a "something you may not have noticed." In fact, I had not noticed it. The words *should* and *need to* were to me what water is to fish: something I swam in 24/7. How could I be aware of something that was always in my experience? I couldn't.

My friend's advice ended at what not to say. For an idea of what to say instead, I turned to a book. Sadly, I don't remember the title or the author, but I can tell you what it said: stop talking about what you should do and start talking about what you want to do. This meant using words such as *I'd like* and *I want* and *It would be great if* and *I've decided*. The author made it sound like switching to these words was as easy as putting on a new pair of shoes. Hardly. Admitting that I wanted something was foreign to a mind accustomed to following rules of how to act. Declaring that something would be great violated an inner commitment to not get my hopes up because things could come crashing down. So flipping words wasn't easy. But I did it, and gradually my language shifted. Having a cue—hearing myself about to say the word *should*—proved to be a great help. As a result, these days the word *should* is rarely heard coming from my lips, and I don't think you'll find it many times in this book. (If you do, you really should not tell me).

I share this story for two reasons. First, it demonstrated for me the challenge and power of flipping words. Second, the act of trying this myself opened me to the idea of using the "flip" approach to handle a more pervasive organizational pastime: grumbling, moaning, and complaining.

Complaining. We all do it. We all listen to others do it. And sometimes we even complain about it. (Can you say *viral?*) In fact, we even have a word that makes complaining sound productive: *venting*. It's such a fine metaphor:

Tanya: Hey, Bob, sounds like you need to vent.

Bob: Yep. Time to open up that gable vent and air out my emotions.

Tanya: And not a moment too soon. It was getting stuffy in there.

Venting is prevalent in most organizations and particularly pervasive in paranoid cultures. When there is a mix of fear and distrust, there is a lot to complain about! Venting is like eating or going to the bathroom: something everyone needs to do to get through the day. Actually, most people are more likely to skip lunch than miss an opportunity to complain. (Go ahead, track this yourself for a week). Some erroneously call it a sign of emotional intelligence and compassionate listening. But that's just rationalizing something that drains the life out of organizations by sucking people into negative moods.

So what do you do when you hear someone else start to complain? This is the million-dollar question. The most common response to complaining is to listen to it, encourage it, and/or add your own tales of woe. The assumption is that this creates camaraderie, but it's camaraderie of the miserable. To use Gottman's terminology, it's *turning toward*, but turning toward negativity.[22]

Another common response is to *turn against* complaint in an attempt to shut it out and shut them up. "Suck it up," you say. "Haven't you said enough about that?" Or, half-jokingly, "Dude, you're bringing me down." (I don't know the female version of Dude, but the same principle applies). All of these potential responses reduce trust and send the complainer off in search of friendlier ears.

Finally, there is *turning away*. When someone complains, you ignore them or change the topic. Or, once you've identified someone as a perpetual complainer (sometimes known as an "energy vampire"), you simply avoid interacting with them. In truly extreme cases, this may be an appropriate response. From a managerial perspective, what do you do when an energy vampire has claimed victims for years without remorse? Either give employees garlic to carry around (hey, it's less expensive than a "mental health" sick day) or find another place for the energy vampire to hang out. Seriously, the only thing worse than an energy vampire employee is an energy vampire manager running performance reviews that involve ranking employees. But we've already nailed that coffin shut, haven't we?

Is there a fourth option, one that sustains mutual trust without creating a caravan of woe? I learned from Robert Kegan and Lisa Lahey[23] that there is. It's called flipping complaints into commitments. The basic idea is that behind every complaint is something you are committed to. If you watch your complaint closely, you'll get a pretty good idea of what you care about.

For example, one senior manager I coached was continuously frustrated with others not following through on their promises. People would promise to do something and then not do it. He brought this up with me constantly. Rather than let him gripe forever or tell him to shut up, I asked him to consider what was behind this complaint. After a moment of reflection, he identified it: a commitment to reliability.

I encouraged him to say this out loud: "I am committed to reliability." Although reluctant at first, he finally got the words out of his mouth. "How did that feel?" I asked. "Awkward," he replied." "Great," I said. "Try it five more times."

He was silent. I realized that my request wasn't clear. "Please try it out five times *now*." "Oh," he replied, and then repeated this declaration five times out loud. As I listened, I sensed that he was getting more comfortable with each iteration. After the last one, I asked him, "So, how was that." He thought for a minute and said, "It's alright. Not bad. I can actually feel this is something I mean. I really am committed to people being reliable."

The entire practice session I just described took less than five minutes. For this manager, the practice presented quite a challenge, no less than the one I experienced in flipping *I should* to *I want*. Fortunately, it was the beginning of a sustained practice. Over several months, he found that every time he acknowledged his commitment to reliability, whether out loud to others or quietly to himself, it energized him. It brought him in touch with what he was moving toward, a space of possibility. This fired him up.

When it comes to flipping complaints to commitments, two points bear repeating. First, it's a great way to shift your mood and create a space of possibility around you. Second, you can't just do it once and expect results. As with every other practice, competence grows through repetition. Going from mediocre to decent to good takes hundreds of repetitions. Going from there to great takes even more.

So how can you start flipping complaints to commitments? I suggest these steps:

1. *Pay attention* to what you're complaining about. A coworker? Your boss? A direct report who seems out to get you? How dreadfully slowly things change in your organization—or how painfully fast? Whatever it is, write it down.

2. Take a few deep breaths and notice: *where is this complaint occupying space in your body?* Where are your muscles tight or pained? Breathe into these areas so you can relax and feel more prepared for the next step.

3. Ask yourself *what do you care about so much* that its absence from your experience is causing you to complain? What are you committed to? Trusting relationships with coworkers? Clear expectations with your boss? Thoughtful change? Whatever it is, write it down. Make sure you start the sentence with, "I am committed to_____." The words matter because they immediately position you not as a victim who complains but as a powerful person who has commitments.

4. *Say it out loud* to a trusted colleague or friend when an opportunity presents itself. (If it's something you're truly committed to, pay attention and there will be boundless opportunities.) It will feel

awkward, but so what? That just means you're a beginner. With practice it will get easier. If you're doubtful about this, skip ahead to the chapter on Visualizing and incorporate your new commitment into the exercise of imagining possibility so that it becomes a reality within you.

5. Over time, *notice when your declaration spontaneously comes out of you.* Pay attention to what that feels like to you and how it impacts others. Appreciate how much less effort it takes today compared to a month ago. Imagine what it might be like to build your conversations around this commitment in the future.

Remember: you may have been raised to complain, but you were born to flip.

CHAPTER 10

ARGUING BETTER

A SURPRISINGLY LARGE percentage of managerial missteps—like ignoring market signals or failing to execute on commitments—are due to mediocre arguing. Arguing, my term for the candid and respectful airing of perspectives, is one of the best ways to test your assumptions, fill in your blind spots, and expand your perspective. Sometimes you'll hear people say, "C'mon folks, stop arguing." Maybe it's my New York roots, but I am very comfortable with arguing. My only beef with arguing is that we don't do it well enough.

While working in North Carolina in the mid 1990s, I saw many examples of people avoiding or stifling their own inclination to argue. They kept their differences to themselves to be polite and remain cordial—at least on the surface. In Oregon, we run a version of this called "Northwest Nice." In both cases, the candid airing of perspectives is missing. It's mediocre arguing by omission.

Then there is mediocre arguing by commission. This occurs in organizations that encourage debate but do it poorly. In the case of paranoid cultures, they do it very poorly. The problem isn't too little airing of opinion but too little learning; not too much deference but too much vehemence; not hidden decisions but poorly grounded decisions; not too much light, but too much heat.

The recipe for mediocre arguing looks something like this:

1. Gather a bunch of strong-willed people together.
2. Give them something to talk about.
3. Provide them with 10-15 years of role modeling the following behaviors: advocating for your own position, preparing your next position while the other person is speaking, and listening only for what you find disagreeable, risky or otherwise suspect.
4. Discourage the use of white boards or flip charts for documenting and clarifying ideas.
5. Schedule their days tightly so they're looking at their laptops half of the time in order to catch up on work.
6. Make the laptop work engaging enough that they aren't too distracted by the discussion but not so engaging that they miss hearing points they find objectionable.
7. If at all possible, promote and reward these people based on individual performance, preferably by ranking them against each other. Even better if the person doing the ranking is in the room.
8. Bake for 90 minutes in a cramped room, preferably with no natural light.

Yes, I know what you're thinking. For a book about possibility, this is a dark and even cynical vision. But that's the point, isn't it? If paranoid organizations weren't so de-energizing and their arguing so mediocre, there would be no need for possibility leadership.

As it turns out, mediocre arguing is a potent force in keeping organizations from realizing their potential. It produces lots of noise but little that is audible; lots of heat but little light. More specifically, the lack of learning between people lowers the quality of decision making. The vehemence of advocacy pushes people apart. And the atmosphere of suspicion and distrust makes it harder to evoke people's best, keep them engaged, and retain top talent.

Possibility leadership calls for very different behaviors and structures around arguing. Some of these involve systemic change that is beyond the scope of this book. But a significant portion of these behaviors is very much in your hands.

Before you use these hands to increase the quality of arguing, I want to disabuse you of a popular notion. Some managers think that productive conversations—the kinds that promote learning and mutual understanding—require you to be *nice* or *soft* or *lose your edge*. This is item #57 on my list of leadership straw men. Although it provides a convenient excuse to keep doing things the same old way, it's an assessment with little grounding. Think about the people you know who can simultaneously describe their perspectives with clarity and power *and* encourage others to do the same, who can hash through disagreements with respect and patience. Would you call these people *weak*?

I don't use the term weak to describe human beings (unless referring to their physical capacities), but if I did, I certainly wouldn't use it to describe someone powerful enough to have a tough, candid, and respectful airing of differences. That just doesn't make sense. In fact, two of the mostly highly regarded corporate CEOs of the past few decades, Jack Welch and Lou Gerstner, were frank and hard-nosed men who were passionate about having vigorous and respectful debate. Both had flaws—we all do—but that didn't stop them from arguing well.

So if you can assume for the moment that learning to argue better is an act of power, then what might you do to increase the quality of your arguing? Here are five suggestions:

1. *Don't confuse assessments with assertions.* People waste enormous amounts of time because they don't know the difference between these two "speech acts." Any time you hear an argument about

who's right and who's wrong, you are seeing this confusion in action. So let's get this clear. Assertions are statements of fact that can either be true or false. Assessments are statements about the quality of something that can be either grounded or ungrounded. *It's 70 degrees outside* is an assertion. You can verify it by looking at a thermometer or weather.com. *It's hot outside* is an assessment. It cannot be true or false because assessments can never be true or false. You can provide evidence to ground your assessment that it's hot, but there is no way to be right. (*Everyone in our group says it's hot outside* is an assertion. You can verify it by asking people.) A huge proportion of arguing in organizations is about whether or not it's true that it's hot outside. People's emotions and identities get wrapped up in being right about something that is not objectively verifiable. What's the alternative? When you are describing your view, call it "my take" or "my assessment." When you are summarizing someone else's, call it "your take" or "your assessment."

2.   *Ground your assessments.* Using words like "take" and "assessment" is an important first step. It can lift a conversation out of miserable confusion and into a space of possibility. The next step is to describe the rationale or data behind your assessments. "Let me tell you why I think it's time to exit this market." "I can think of three solid reasons why Julie would be a better hire for this role than John." These explanations of "the why" are as important as they are rare, particularly in the middle of heated discussion. They are important because they allow you to test your assumptions and help others understand why you see things the way you do. They're rare in heated arguing because they involve reason, and the reptile brain that gets activated at such moments is by definition not reasonable. (Ever met a reasonable alligator?) Even when you're not emotionally triggered, grounding assessments can seem both difficult and risky—difficult because

you haven't actually thought through your reasoning; and risky because revealing your assumptions allows others to challenge them. The good news? Grounding your assessments makes you simultaneously more persuasive and more trustworthy.

3. *Invite others to ground their assessments.* When someone tells you their perspective, it's tempting to immediately reply by advocating for your own, perhaps even interrupting them in the process. Stop doing this. Seriously, your default response isn't helping you, the other person, or the conversation. Instead, invite your colleague to ground her assessment. "Madhu, it sounds like your assessment is that it's time to exit this market. I'm sure you've put a lot of thought into this. Could you please walk me through your reasoning." Or, "I know you discussed this assessment a few months ago but a lot has changed since then. Could you help me understand your thinking behind this today?" By the way, the phrase *help me understand* is an absolute gold mine. It positions you as—and transforms you into—someone trying to learn rather than someone trying to critique.

4. *Make it visual.* For over twenty years I've been using flip charts, white boards, and sticky notes to facilitate conversations. These simple tools work because they give groups a "public memory" of what's been said. They're visual, and visual learning works. It amazes me how many teams ignore such tools or use them poorly. In most cases, people are simply following the habits of their cultures. In some cases, that means "leading by PowerPoint," which is as effective as exercising by watching TV. In other cases, that means relying on people's ears to have superpowers that make visual learning unnecessary. Either way, the cultural habits are so entrenched that it takes courage to walk up to the white board and start capturing ideas. Fortunately, such actions yield real dividends. When you see your ideas—

particularly your assessments and the rationale behind them—on a white board, you're more likely to "feel heard." When others see those ideas, they are more likely to understand your thinking and create genuine questions to ask. Then you can have a healthy and vigorous argument.

5. *Put peripheral topics in the "parking lot."* It's hard enough to have one good conversation at any given time, much less several. That's why when peripheral topics emerge, I suggest you put them in the "parking lot," ideally, on a white board or flip chart. This keeps the group focused on the topic at hand and allows the person who brings up the "peripheral" idea to have confidence that the group will return to their topic later.

In summary, a big part of leadership is arguing. Possibility leadership is about arguing better.

Chapter 11

Telling Stories

"A STORY NOT only expresses motivation, it motivates. It not only describes learning, it embodies, reflects and causes learning. Telling the story over and over makes it real. As the group's story evolves and grows, it becomes a vehicle through which the group can act 'as if' and bring new ideas and worlds into being."[24]

--Lisa Marshall, *Speak The Truth and Point to Hope*

Storytelling has always been a core part of leadership. But only recently have the people who study, teach, and coach leadership begun to talk about it.

What do we know about telling stories that is relevant to possibility leadership? Let me summarize what I've learned:

1.   Stories can be incredibly powerful because of how they affect the human brain, and they comprise a large part of people's everyday conversations.

2. All managers tell stories, but their stories vary widely in quality and relevance.

3. Good stories share a common structure. They have protagonists, challenges, conflicts, and resolutions. They have beginnings, middles, and ends. Sometimes they have villains.

4. Good leadership stories consciously include listeners as protagonists. Everyone feels like an actor in the story.

5. Great leadership stories connect people's everyday experiences to the strategic challenges of the organization.

6. Great leadership stories also evoke positive emotion and inspire people to take action.

7. Great leadership storytelling requires more than just a great story. Other essential elements include the physical presence (voice, facial expressions, body posture, and movement) of the storyteller and use of visuals, location, and timing.

8. Great leadership storytelling isn't the only way to express a story. The other option is to embody it.

Embodying a story of possibility leadership is what I teach best. It's what this book is about. If you're interested in learning more about how to *construct and tell* great leadership stories, consider these resources:

- Nancy Duarte's book *Resonate: Present Visual Stories that Transform Audiences.* Duarte introduces a powerful methodology for giving persuasive presentations. My favorite part is her recommendation that speakers invite audiences into a tension between "what is" and "what could be"—not once but multiple times in a talk.

- Howard Gardner's book *Leading Minds: An Anatomy of Leadership.* Famous for his theory of multiple intelligences, Gardner writes about several prominent leaders in business, government, and academia whose success derives in large part from the stories they communicate and embody. Gardner claims that the most effective stories are those that appeal to the "unschooled" (6-year-old) mind that thinks in terms of right and wrong.

- A TED Talk by Hans Rosling called "New Insights on Poverty." Rosling is a genius at bringing numbers to life with flair and amazing visuals. He is an answer to the question: how do you tell a great story with data?

- Stephen Few's books *Show Me the Numbers: Designing Tables and Graphs to Enlighten* and *Information Dashboard Design*. Once you've read Few, you'll be embarrassed by the quality of charts in your organization, learn to instantly recognize "chart junk," and become way more adept at telling stories with numbers.

- *Beyond Bullet Points: Using Microsoft Office Powerpoint 2007 to Create Presentations that Inform, Motivate, and Inspire* by Cliff Atkinson. Detailed tips on planning your slides, creating storyboards, adding graphics, and delivering your presentation. The author also happens to be a friend and a man of great emotional depth.

- *Three Stories Leaders Tell* by Chris Cavanaugh-Simmons. This book by a highly regarded Silicon Valley executive coach shows how to construct three types of leadership stories: "Who am I?" "Who are We" and "Where are We Going?"

- *For All Time: A Complete Guide to Writing Your Family History* by Charles Kempthorne. How do you mine your life for stories that could be useful to your organization? This book is a great guide.

If you had to choose between telling great stories and embodying a great story, I'd encourage you to select the latter. However, if you have the inclination to improve at both, these resources are a great place to start.

CHAPTER 12

LISTENING LIKE A MASTER

"PEOPLE NEED THE ability to listen very openly to other people. Most of us tend to listen with a bias to what we already know and value."[25]

—Carol Weber, Darden School of Business, University of Virginia

The first five outer practices for possibility leadership all involve listening. Now it's time to hone in on what it takes to listen like a master. This is the first time I've used the word *master* in this book. This is deliberate. My intent is to emphasize how important it is to listen with extraordinary skill, because if you can do this, you can do everything else. Listening like a master allows you to see possibilities where others see problems, know when and how to turn toward others, appreciate the commitments behind people's complaints, understand divergent perspectives, make grounded assessments, construct powerful stories, and appreciate what makes others tick. These abilities, in turn, help you make better decisions, build better teams, retain top talent, and foster cultures of trust and possibility. If you listen like a master and others around you do, too, the paranoid qualities of your organization's culture will melt away as quickly as ice cubes in a pot of boiling water.

These are bold statements, wouldn't you say? After all, isn't listening a "soft," unimportant skill not worthy of academic research, much less the valuable time of practicing managers? Aren't you already a good enough listener? And even if you wanted to become a better listener, how much can you really do to change things? These are all important questions, so I'll handle them in sequence.

WHAT MAKES LISTENING SO IMPORTANT?

It is true that the amount of research on listening in organizations is scant. This is due partly to its reputation as a "soft" skill and partly to the logistical difficulty of measuring listening quality. My own belief in listening as a pivotal leadership practice stems largely from two sources: my experience helping leaders listen more skillfully and my efforts to become a better listener myself. In both cases, I've seen anecdotal (if not rigorous statistical) evidence that listening pays big time.

Let's begin with a personal example. When I was 22 years old and in my first adult job, the company that hired me was a national consulting and training firm led by a handful of seasoned and very talented consultants. I was the junior guy trying hard but in way over my head. Salient fact: the man who preceded me in the position left it to direct the training function for a mid-sized American city. In contrast, I was still trying to figure out how to function without professors and grades.

Perhaps the hardest part of the job was responding to my boss's requests and feedback. At the time, I thought he was overly demanding and critical. In retrospect, I realize that I was listening to him through a powerful filter that went like this: does he trust me, or doesn't he trust me? No matter what he did or said, my mind and body interpreted it as a response to this question. Because he set high standards and was not shy about letting me know when I didn't meet them, my reactions to him were often negative and defensive. In phone conversations, I froze, my body unable to tolerate the difficult physical sensations from the perceived attack. In written correspondence, a medium with which I was historically more comfortable, I concocted long and elaborate arguments in favor of my positions coupled with emotional pleas for him to take it easier on me. The Ice Man by phone and the Criminal Defense Lawyer by email and fax. That was how I listened, so that was how I rolled.

I could have maintained this listening filter for the ensuing twenty years. It's unlikely I would have become an executive coach, but I could have done many other things reasonably well. Not admirably and not happily, but at a level of adequacy that would pay the bills.

Fortunately, this is not what happened. When I was in my early 30s, I became aware of this listening filter and the pervasive impact it had in my life. To be clear, I call this realization "fortunate," but it was far from pleasant. Who wants to discover that a huge percentage of his experience is driven by a preoccupation with whether or not others trust him? Not me. That's not who I took myself to be. In fact, it was a bit like you would feel if you learned that you've had bad breath for a decade and never knew about it: ashamed at how you'd been and embarrassed that you were oblivious to it.

The fortunate part is what happened next. I found a teacher, James Flaherty,[26] who showed me what was happening and taught me to approach this matter with compassion, not criticism. I found friends who were willing to put up with my shenanigans and support me in reducing their number and severity. And I started to practice new ways of listening.

To make a long story short, I spent three years rigorously observing the pervasiveness and impact of my trust/distrust listening filter; three years imagining what it would be like to own, rather than be owned by, this filter; five years practicing conscious self-correction whenever the filter interfered with my listening; and two years experiencing the filter less as an enemy and more as that crazy relative that shows up once a year at the holidays with strange gifts and stranger jokes.

The result of all this effort? Not just higher quality listening, but a more frequent experience of ease, confidence, and inner strength.

But enough about me.

Let's turn now to an organizational example, one based on composites of real people I've coached:

You are a Senior Vice President in a Fortune 500 company. Two middle managers are giving a presentation to you about dramatic shifts in the industry. They describe these shifts as major threats to the company's core line of products and suggest new strategic directions. Now, you may not know it consciously, but you are wired to listen to this presentation through a particular filter. Like all filters, it allows certain information to go through and blocks off the rest. Your filter works as follows: will this make me look strong or weak? So, as you listen, this is 75 percent of what you are paying attention to even though it's less than 1 percent of what's actually happening.

If you're unaware of this filter, it owns you. You shut these managers' insights out of your awareness because taking them seriously is an admission of weakness. After all, would a strong executive need a bunch of middle managers to tell him what's happening in the industry?

On the other hand, let's say you are aware of your listening filter. At the very moment you start to disregard the managers' perspective, you catch yourself listening through the strength/weakness filter. "Oh, there I go again," you think to yourself. This moment of awareness allows you to listen deeply to the presentation and appreciate the substance behind it. This does not mean you believe everything you hear or accept the presenters' recommendations as given. It means you are strikingly more likely to take what you hear seriously and integrate it into your own thinking. Instead of being owned by your listening filter, you own the filter. Ironically, freeing yourself from the strength/weakness dichotomy makes you a stronger leader.

That's you. Now let's introduce Sasha. She is one of the middle managers preparing to present to you. As she meets with her colleague to outline the presentation, she starts to get anxious. As the colleague walks through the signals of industry transformation, Sasha's mind imagines all the ways her presentation will fail if she actually describes these: You will lash out at her angrily—or quietly seethe in a way that gets the same message across. She will feel humiliated. Her own manager will get angry. She will be fired or, at best, demoted. These thoughts filter how she listens as she prepares for the conversation.

Now, here's the point around which everything else pivots: is Sasha aware of this listening filter? If not, she does everything she can to prevent these dangers. Rather than framing her insights in a way you will understand, she tries to take these insights out of the presentation entirely.

On the other hand, let's say Sasha is aware of her listening filter. She catches herself imagining worst-case scenarios and self-corrects. She realizes those scenarios are assessments, not the truth. She looks for evidence that alternative assessments may come true. And she is more likely to give you the powerful presentation you need to hear.

What's going on in this story? The ability of two leaders to have a constructive conversation that moves the company's strategy forward depends largely on whether these leaders recognize what keeps them from fully listening. If either you or Sasha is unaware of your listening filter, the company will miss a great opportunity to reconsider its place in the market. If Sasha goes soft on the presentation, then you won't learn about her insights, much less benefit from them. If Sasha tells it as she sees it but you filter out the vital message, you'll leave that meeting thinking you know everything you need to know—a blind spot, to say the least. Given your influence on other senior leaders, the company may miss the boat strategically. Given the weight of your power in Sasha's experience, she may decide to never again take such a risk. Who knows how much time will pass before a similar opportunity arises?

On the other hand, if both you and Sasha are aware of your listening filters, things will unfold in a dramatically different fashion. The exchange between you will be focused and fruitful. You, Sasha, and the company will gain.

AREN'T YOU ALREADY A GOOD ENOUGH LISTENER?

Thinking that you are already a good enough listener rests on two premises:

1. Being a good listener is sufficient. There is no need to shoot for mastery.
2. You are already a good listener

Let's tackle the sufficiency assumption first. Part of me agrees with this statement. In a world of mediocre listening—even the best intended of us have strong filters that block out relevant insights—isn't good listening good enough?

Well, good enough for what? For good leadership? For moderately competent leadership? Well, yes, of course it is. But I don't think that's what you're shooting for.

Now, onto the second premise. For sake of argument, let's assume that being a good listener is sufficient. Do you believe you are a good listener? If so, what evidence can you present to ground this assessment? As it turns out, research by Cornell University suggests that most managers overestimate their own listening skills.[27] If you think you're great, you're likely good. If you think you're good, you're likely decent or mediocre. Listening is one of those skills whose quality becomes apparent only when truly put to the test. It's just like humor and singing. You think you're funny because whenever you tell a joke, your mother thinks it's hilarious and your ten-year-old kid laughs hysterically. Then you say the same thing in a meeting at work and you get nothing. Try it at open mike night at the comedy club and you'll be walking home with bananas smeared on your shirt. As for singing, unless you have a great voice, you will *always* sound better in the shower than at the karaoke party. Being skilled at listening works the same way.

HOW MUCH CAN YOU TRULY IMPROVE YOUR LISTENING?

You can improve your listening a great deal under two conditions:

1. You're willing to deliberately practice over a substantial period of time.
2. Your practice includes not just mechanics of listening, but also working on the heart of what gets in the way of your listening.

By this point in the book, you've figured out that I am fond of deliberate practice, so let's talk about *what* to practice to achieve listening mastery. In the story about Sasha delivering a presentation to you, what mattered most was your awareness of your listening filter. As it turns out, you'll find very little about listening filters in most books and classes about listening. What you'll find is a great deal on the mechanics of listening: where to look at someone (just above the nose), how to hold your head (slightly to the side and occasionally nodding), and what sounds to make ("Hmmm," "Yes," and "I see").

There's nothing wrong with these tips. I use them myself. But they provide only a small part of the guidance you need to achieve listening mastery. What they leave out is a response to—or even an acknowledgment of—the most vital question about listening: what gets in the way of good listening?

As we've already seen, everyone listens *for* certain things and screens out the rest. Even if two people hear the same thing, they interpret what they hear differently based upon what they are listening for. These people may share the same physical world, but they carry in their minds very different worlds of interpretation—different world views. There's nothing wrong with listening through a filter—it's how our brains have been wired. What matters is whether or not we are aware of this filter.

What are the specific things you listen for? What are all the other things that this filter screens out?

This is likely new territory for you, so let me provide a simple map. For the sake of this exploration, assume that there are nine listening filters—nine broad patterns of what people screen in and screen out of their attention. Each person, including you, has access to most of these filters some of the time but tends to use a single filter disproportionately more of the time. When you discover yours, think of it as your "home base" or "center of gravity" filter.[28]

Here are the nine filters:

- Am I being criticized? Am I right or wrong about this?
- Am I being appreciated for the help I've given?
- Am I getting credit for my achievements? Or could this negatively affect others' impression of me?
- Does this person see how unique I am?
- Is this going to drain my energy and resources?
- Am I being distrusted? What could go wrong here?
- Is this situation exciting or boring? How can I plan for more fun?
- Who is in charge here? Who is weak and needs my protection?
- Is there harmony here or conflict?

I share this list not so you can identify your filter—that takes more investigation—but to display the wide range of filters that different people have. I hope this encourages you to do the work it takes to discover your "home base" filter so you can develop a deeper awareness of it and reduce its power over you. (I'll discuss ways to identify your filter in the chapter on "healing your Achilles Heel.")

Once you identify your primary listening filter, the next step is to do a few simple things a large number of times:

- *Observe the presence of your listening filter* in your experience—all the ways it shows up (physically, emotionally, cognitively) and the impact this has on you and others.

- *Start to question* the necessity of having this listening filter dominate your experience at all times and in all situations. Are there occasions when perhaps it is less necessary?

- *Experiment with naming* your listening filter when you become aware of it and noticing how this affects your response to situations.

- As your listening filter becomes an object in your awareness, practice *putting yourself in other people's shoes* as you are listening to them. Feel the sounds enter your ears. Sense the movement of your breath enter your lungs. Feel yourself connected to them, perhaps by imagining a chord of light connecting your heart to theirs. (This last one is a bona fide Jedi Mind Trick. It will give you superhuman powers of understanding.)

Here's to listening like a master.

CHAPTER 13

ASKING GREAT QUESTIONS

THROUGHOUT THE PREVIOUS chapters, I've emphasized the importance of questions, both the ones you ask yourself and the ones you ask others. Now let's put this topic front and center.

I want to start by assuming that you're sold on the value of asking great questions. Fair enough?

Excellent. Now we can explore what constitutes a great question and how to incorporate more great questions into your conversational repertoire.

My initial exposure to asking great questions came during that first job out of college that I discussed in the last chapter. My company consulted to organizations in health care and higher education. I was given responsibility for behind-the-scenes work like conducting phone interviews and summarizing data. Sensing my anxiety about interviewing medical school faculty and administrators, my boss gave me the following advice: "Ask a lot of dumb questions. You'll learn more. If you're afraid that this will make you seem dumb, then tell people you're going to ask them a lot of dumb questions." When I asked him what he meant by "dumb," he said "open-ended." So that is what I did, and it worked well. Not once did one of my 50-year-old interviewees say, "Hey, kid, what do you think you're doing interviewing me?" On the contrary, the humbler (and crisper) my questions, the richer the responses they gave me.

This experience taught me three lessons. First, the most powerful questions are often about obvious things that, until now, nobody has had the curiosity or temerity to ask. Second, people like to be asked open-ended questions and given a *lot* of time to respond. Interrupting is bad. Keeping your mouth shut during awkward silences is good. Finally, even a nervous and inexperienced kid can ask great questions, so if you either have experience or lack nerves, there's no excuse for not raising your game.

In the twenty years since I started that first job, I've conducted more formal interviews than I can recall. Asking powerful questions has ceased to be a conscious practice and is now an unconscious habit. That's not to say I don't ask weak and ineffective questions from time to time. I do. But constructing and asking solid questions is now a core part of my identity and one of a few things for which people consistently acknowledge me (sometimes to say "Amiel, cut it out with all the questions!")

Let's talk about what constitutes a great question—or, more specifically, what constitutes asking a great question, since the question itself is only part of the package. As with listening, learning the mechanics of constructing and asking questions is necessary but not sufficient. Equally important are underlying factors like the intention and mood behind your question. In the remaining part of this chapter, I'll share what I've learned about the content of questions and the intention and mood we bring to asking them.

THE CONTENT OF A QUESTION

I used to spend a lot of time thinking about what questions to ask someone. Then I discovered that constructing questions can be relatively simple. The trick is to identify a small set of phrases that are consistently effective at evoking thoughtful responses from others and then use them as often as possible. I think of these as *power phrases* because when incorporated into questions, they elicit powerful responses.

Below are my favorite power phrases, categorized based upon the three types of conversations introduced earlier: conversations for relationship, conversations for possibility, and requests, a core part of conversations for action.

Conversations for Relationship

In conversations for relationships, success is understanding what matters to the other person and helping them understand what matters to you.

- What did you like best about____?
- What did you like least about___?
- What was that like for you?
- Can you help me understand____?
- Can you tell me more about____?
- What's your take on_____?
- What makes this important to you?
- What would_____ [success, happiness, an ideal job, a fun evening on the town, etc.] look like to you?
- If you had to change one thing about____, what would you change?
- If I were to ask you_____, what would you say?

The first time I consciously used some of these questions outside of work was in 1994. I found myself living in a six-bedroom house in Chapel Hill, North Carolina with only one other housemate. He was the chief tenant and therefore responsible for selecting other people to join us. Worried about who he might pick, I offered to run the housemate interview process. My goal was to get to know applicants' habits and preferences without first revealing what I was looking for. This would prevent them from selling me on what they thought I wanted. I held eight or nine interviews for four spots, and each one became a conversation for relationship. Here is what I asked:

- What are you looking for in a house?
- What are you looking for in terms of housemates?
- When you've had housemates in the past, what has worked well for you? What has not?
- If you were to name one thing that would make you want to move out of a house because it was so unpleasant, what would that be?
- If I were to ask your past housemates to describe you, what three adjectives would they use?

It was amazing to observe how much people revealed about themselves and how greatly this helped us in assessing them for fit. Granted, some people's actual preferences likely differed from their stated preferences, but for the most part, their answers were predictive of their behaviors. In the end, all four housemates we selected ended up being excellent fits.

Conversations for Possibility

In conversations for possibility, success entails exploring a possible future scenario or decision *without critique* in order to experience what that future may be like and what benefits it can bring. For example, you could ask:

- What if we were to___? What might that look and sound like?
- If we were to_____, what positive results would you expect to see? What new possibilities would open up?
- Assume for a moment that____were possible. What conditions would need to be present for it to work?
- Who else might be interested in this? What would they be excited about?
- What if we were to combine____with____—how might that play out?

Requests (A Part of Conversations for Action)

In requests, success involves speaking to a specific person (rather than to an amorphous group), establishing clear conditions for satisfaction (exactly what the other person needs to do for you to feel satisfied), setting a specific timeframe, embodying a mood of possibility (as opposed to resentment or resignation), conveying that *Yes* is not the only acceptable response (also acceptable: *No*, a counteroffer, or a promise to get back to you later), and actually speaking the request (as opposed to just thinking it).

It takes a lot to make a good request! That's why the question you ask as part of the request is so important. As you read the list of questions below, please keep in mind that the most effective phrasing depends entirely on the situation: what are you requesting? Who are you asking (and what's the power relationship between you)? How interested do you think they'll be in fulfilling the request? Is this something that they'll see as a chore, or something they'll actually enjoy doing? How important and urgent is this request to you? The specifics of the situation will dictate the best way to phrase the question.

- Will you_____?
- Will you agree to_____?
- Would you be willing to_____?
- Would you like to_____?
- Would you be interested in_____?
- Do you have any objection to_____?
- Will this work for you?
- What will it take to make this work for you?
- If I_____, would you be willing to_____?

Disclosure: my number one favorite phrase for making requests is *Would you be willing to_____?* This conveys respect by implying that the other person has the will—and freedom—to accept or decline. It also avoids the trap of pointing to what the other person likes or wants. You're not asking *Would you like to do this?* You're asking *Would you be willing to do this?* Finally, this phrase works in a wide variety of situations with a broad range of people. Such multiplicity of use comes in handy when you want to practice asking questions and have the mental bandwidth for only one approach. You want to pick the one you can use everywhere, right?

THE MOOD AND INTENTION BEHIND A QUESTION

Ten years ago, I gave a workshop to a group of fellow executive coaches about how to avoid "conversational breakdowns." I talked primarily about which words were effective and which words might get you into trouble. The group enjoyed the distinctions I made and seemed animated by the topic. Then my friend, Steve March, raised his hand and politely said, "Amiel, what you're saying about language seems very important. However, I wonder how effective any of this will be without the right intention." The comment caught me by surprise, not because it was a new concept, but because it was one I had accidentally omitted from the workshop *despite how important I knew it to be.* At that moment, I made a commitment to myself that whenever speaking or writing about language, I would always talk about the mood and intention behind the words.

Thank you, Steve.

Now, let's assume you've become highly competent at constructing questions. What difference does the mood and intention behind your question make?

Mood

Let's start with mood, the emotional field in which you regularly live. Mood is to emotion as climate is to weather. In the context of asking questions, your mood influences both you—the energy and integrity you bring to the question—and the other person—the emotional space they experience while hearing your question. For example, consider three different moods you can have while making a request:

In the first case, you walk up to someone in a mood of resentment. Your face is angry, and your breath is shallow. You're not a happy camper. When you reach out to them to make a request, what happens? Odds are good that the other person will think, "She sure has a chip on her shoulder. Not sure I want to get involved in that."

In the second case, you approach that same person in a mood of resignation. Your shoulders sag, and your voice is flat. When you make the very same request using exactly the same words, what happens now? It's likely that the other person will feel your flat affect and low energy in their body. Even if they like you and want to help, they'll feel little inspiration to sign on.

In the third case, you approach that individual in a mood of possibility. Your face, voice, and body all convey strength and excitement. Now you make the exact same request. Do you expect the person to respond differently than in the first two cases? Undoubtedly yes, because your physical and emotional energy evokes something positive in them.

Mood has a similar impact on conversations for relationship and possibility. The emotional space you create either opens or closes the space of possibility between you and the other person.

Intention

How does intention differ from mood? Your intention is the specific outcome you want from asking a question. More often than not, your intention lives below your field of awareness. You think you're asking a question, but in reality you are playing another game with its own peculiar goals and rules. What sorts of games do people play while asking questions? I've played all of these games myself, so here are some examples from my own experience:

- When I was 23 years old, I met with my boss for my first-ever performance review. After telling me how much he enjoyed my work, he asked, "So, Amiel, do you want to make a case for how much you want to be paid, or do you want me to tell you how much you will be paid?" The question confused me, but I interpreted it literally and proceeded to argue for a particular salary increase. My boss was frustrated by my response. An uncomfortable 40-minute argument followed. Later I realized that my boss's intention wasn't to hear my preference about salary, but to communicate that he had already made a decision.

- When I was 29, I had coffee with a semi-famous leadership consultant who knew everybody. He was a generation older than me. Going into the meeting, I told him, "I'm not looking for connections. I just want to talk with you." During the meeting, I asked him a series of questions about his work. In theory, it was a conversation for relationship. In reality, what I really wanted was for him to introduce me to people he knew. He eventually figured this out and called me on it. I felt ashamed.

- During a phone conversation, a close relative interrupted me multiple times without apology. I got angry. "You continue to interrupt me," I said, "and I'm getting very frustrated. What's it going to take for you to stop?" I didn't care about his response and didn't want to hear it. I wanted to drill home how angry I was while appearing reasonable and mature.

- My wife had been out of town for a week. I'd been home with the kids. The night before she flew back, I asked her, "How would you say this trip has been for you?" I cared about her answer, but I already knew she'd had a great time. What I secretly hoped was that she'd thank me (again!) for holding down the fort. This was exactly what she did.

In each of these examples, the person asking the question is up to something. They don't say it, wouldn't admit it if asked, and may not even be aware of it. But it's right there below the surface, and the other person feels it. In none of these cases is the person's intention to learn from the other person or even invite an authentic response. Instead, curiosity is trumped by fear, manipulation, anger, or resentment.

Hopefully, these examples give you a sense of the range of intentions that can lay behind any question. Here is a back-of-envelope model called *Amiel's Ratings of Intentions Behind Questions:*

- A: Asked with curiosity and openness to having your own assumptions overturned
- A-: Asked with curiosity and the hope that your assumptions will be confirmed
- B: Asked to get an objective response
- C: Intended to gently point out defects or steer in a direction
- D: Intended to badger, criticize or force in a particular direction
- F: Intended to humiliate or cause other forms of damage

79

CHAPTER 14

NEUTRALIZING ENEMIES

HOW HEALTHY ARE your relationships with the people most pivotal to your work? What would healthier look like, and how can you take your relationships there?

Many people don't ask these questions. Leaders in paranoid organizations never ask these questions, because what's the point? Their relationships are what they are. They're not going to change, and if they do they'll get worse, not better. As people often say to me, "Charles and I can't stand each other, and we will never be best friends, so what's the point?"

At first this sounds reasonable. Charles likely will never be your best friend. But, it has all the signs and flaws of classic straw man argument. What you're really saying is this: if a lousy relationship cannot suddenly morph into a great friendship, then why bother improving it?

As though mediocrity and greatness were the only two options.

When you put it that way, the whole argument sounds ridiculous, yet literally millions of people use it every day to avoid improving relationships. The cost is substantial: toxic relationships that don't improve remain toxic. They drain more time and energy from organizations than just about anything else. And, to repeat the key point, they don't need to be great to be better than toxic. Very often, a neutral and respectful relationship will do just fine.

This is why this practice is called *neutralizing* enemies: invest the time to improve the lousy relationships until they're at least neutral and respectful. And, while you're at it, to improve the other relationships that truly matter. Let's walk through the steps for doing this.

WHICH RELATIONSHIPS ARE IMPORTANT?

To start, make a list of the relationships that are obviously important to you: your boss, your direct reports, your peers, and any internal or external customers. Now add to this list the names of people who have helped you make something happen in the past, those who could block what you're doing, and those who "own" key resources or have the ear of the people who do. We'll call these your important relationships.

WHAT IS THE CURRENT QUALITY OF THESE RELATIONSHIPS?

Here comes the fun part. For each person on the list, make an assessment of the health of your relationship. Use the following scale:

1. *Toxic*—neither of you can be in the room with the other without feeling ill.
2. *Negative*—when you're around each other, it isn't relaxing and can feel unpleasant.
3. *Neutral/Respectful*—no warm fuzzies but also no ill will.
4. *Positive*—you enjoy each other and have a mutual respect.
5. *Great Vibe*—being around each other is easy and effortless. Your conversations "flow" and fill you with positive energy.

WHICH RELATIONSHIPS ARE TRULY PIVOTAL?

Now it's time to focus. If you were to pick three to five relationships to invest in improving over the next six months, which ones would you choose? I suggest you use a single criterion for making this decision:

Which relationships, if improved, will have the greatest positive impact on your ability to accomplish your goals and fulfill your purpose?

Notice that I'm not asking you to assess the value of a relationship. I'm asking you to assess the value of the improvement in a relationship. The ones that rate most highly are your pivotal relationships.

WHAT DOES AN IMPROVED RELATIONSHIP LOOK LIKE?

Take a look at this list of three to five pivotal relationships. Ask yourself, how healthy would you like each relationship to be in 6 months? What would an improvement in each look like? There are two rules to remember when thinking about this:

1. The relationship improves at least one point on the quality scale.
2. Every relationship ends up at least at Neutral/Respectful.

WHAT CAN YOU DO TO IMPROVE THE RELATIONSHIP?

The specific steps you take to improve each relationship depend upon many factors: the current and desired future health of the relationship, your strengths and style of building relationship, the other person's preferred communication style and medium, the intensity of your current work together, the nature of your working relationship (peers, boss, direct support, etc.), and the specific history you have with each other. Nonetheless, there is a handful of practices worth considering regardless of your particular situation:

- *Apologize.* Have you done anything in the past that hurt the other person? Have you ever apologized for it? A simple apology given with sincerity and heart can go a long way.

- *Say thanks.* Keep an eye open for little things the person does that you appreciate. These could be things they've done for years that you've never noticed or acknowledged. Thank them for these actions. Be sure to mention precisely what it is you appreciate and the specific positive impact it has on you.

- *Have a conversation for relationship.* Schedule time to find out what's important to the other person and reveal what you care about. Speak genuinely and listen openly. If you already know that they like Thai food, suggest having this conversation over lunch at a Thai restaurant.

- *Turn toward* them. Every micro-interaction you have with them is an opportunity to make small improvements in your relationship by turning toward them.

- *Stop doing something* that bothers them. Everyone has pet peeves, so this person likely has one related to you. Find out what it is and stop doing it.

- *Acknowledge changes* they've made. If you've started to change how you interact with this other person, it's quite possible they will change how they behave toward you. When they do something positive, however small, appreciate it. Don't contrast it to what they used to do but simply acknowledge their effort and the positive result.

If you take these steps and adapt them to your situation, you can neutralize your enemies and strengthen your ties with your friends.

This is a good time to review the eight outer practices of possibility leadership and ask yourself, which of these could have the biggest impact on my leadership? Remember that I'm encouraging you to select one outer practice and focus on it like a laser beam.

The next step is to get familiar with the seven *inner* practices of possibility leadership. What can you do when nobody else is looking to increase your capacity to lead others into a space of possibility? This question brings us to Part Three.

PART THREE

THE INNER PRACTICES

CHAPTER 15

VISUALIZING

IN THE 1988 World Series, Kirk Gibson hit one of the most memorable home runs of all time. With two outs in the bottom of the ninth inning and the Los Angeles Dodgers trailing 4-3, Gibson pinch hit a game-winning homer. What is remarkable is that he did it with two injured legs—the man could barely walk—against one of the top relievers in the game, Dennis Eckersley, and only after fouling off multiple pitches with the count at two strikes. You've probably seen the famous video of him hobbling around the bases and pumping his fist into the air.

What you may not know is that right before Gibson hit that home run, he visualized it in his mind. Literally. He created a mental image of himself knocking the ball over the fence. And then he did it.

This visualization practice had been part of Gibson's repertoire for years. I first hear about it in 1984 when he played for my hometown team, the Detroit Tigers. In that World Series, he hit a game-clinching homer in the 8th inning, his second of the game, against another amazing relief pitcher, Goose Gossage. In an interview after the game, he talked about how he had visualized the homer while he was standing at the plate. I remember thinking to myself, "That's weird, but, wow, did it work!"

Just as it has in many other fields, including business. Visualizing success is a proven method for elevating performance. It operates by creating within you a scaffolding for what you will then create outside of you. Visualizing is part of preparing for performance. More importantly, it is a practice you repeat over and over again until it comes naturally to you. By the time Gibson hit his climactic homers in the 1984 and 1988 World Series, he had been visualizing them for years.

What experiences have you had visualizing positive possibilities? In what domains of your life have you used visualization? Sports? Academic performance? Giving a speech? Entering a difficult conversation?

I invite you to consider the impact that visualization can have on your leadership. Consider the outer practices of possibility leadership. How might visualization support you in taking on these practices and thereby elevating your game? Let's say you decide to have more conversations for possibility with your peers. What would it be like to quietly envision yourself having one? Can you picture it now? Or let's assume you want to argue better by getting really good at asking others to ground their assessments. Can you create a picture in your mind's eye of what it would feel like to do this and the impact it would have on the conversation?

As you dip your toe into these examples, you may be reminded of my earlier challenge to identify your purpose. In both cases, you are acting from a place of volition or conscious choice. However, there is an important difference. Your purpose is what you stand for now and forever. Visualization puts you in touch with a particular experience involving particular people at a specific point in time. For example, it is energizing to declare my current purpose, developing great leaders for clean technology and sustainability. However, this declaration conveys nothing of what my experience will be like in the future. Nor does it help me see myself having amazing conversations for possibility with the leaders I intend to serve. Both of these require acts of visualization.

So how do you do it? There are a number of effective methods. Popular ones include doing closed-eyed visualization, drawing pictures, and writing mock future news headlines describing in past tense what you've accomplished. I recommend trying them all to find what works best for you. First, try this simple exercise you can do right now in less than five minutes:

As you think about your current work, please fill in the blanks:

- Wouldn't it be nice if_____?
- Wouldn't it be cool if_____?
- Wouldn't it be great if_____?

I recently assigned this exercise to an executive I'm coaching who has a big job involving enormous complexity and pressure. In three minutes, he came up with five items, all of them things he would really love to see happen yet that he had not to that point articulated. What allowed him to do this? I'd love to say it was my presence, but I'd put my money on the framing of the sentence. There's something about *Wouldn't it be nice if* that frees up your energy and jump starts your imagination. If you're feeling resignation about what's possible, it lifts you up out of that. If you're feeling resentment toward people getting in your way, that, too, falls by the wayside. Better yet, there's no promise specified or implied by the statement. You are trying on the idea, not making a commitment to it. This evokes a positive mood. You feel lighter and more open. This is precisely what happened with the executive who did the exercise.

Unfortunately, not everyone follows the instructions. More than half of the people who try this exercise verbally skip the all-important initial phrase and simply fill in the blank.

Overheard recently at a conference room near you:

Amiel: "OK, Ralph. Tell me what you came up with."

Ralph: "The organization can get through this rough patch without losing anyone or laying anyone off."

Amiel: "Ralph, my good friend, you've accidentally left out the first part of the sentence, *Wouldn't it be nice if.*"

Ralph: "Oh, yeah, you're right. It did feel fragmented. Here goes again: Wouldn't it be nice if the organization could get through this rough patch without losing anyone or laying anyone off."

Amiel: "Now, what's that like to say?"

Ralph: "Better. More positive. More energy."

Amiel: "Great. Wouldn't it be nice if you could learn to do this all the time?"

Ralph: "Very clever, Amiel! But, to answer your question, yes, it would be very nice. It would be great."

I invite you to try this yourself. Pick one of the outer practices:

Wouldn't it be nice if_____?

Chapter 16

Seeing Patterns

NOW THAT YOU'RE learning to see future realities that exist within you, let's try something different. How about seeing past realities that exist outside of you? In particular, let's look for two kinds of patterns:

- Patterns of behavior in your organization's interaction with the marketplace that reveal emergent organizational strategies.
- Patterns that reveal your team's strengths.

The capacity to *see patterns* is an inner practice that can bolster possibility leadership in numerous ways. For example, identifying your organization's emergent strategies (which we will define shortly) gives you material for compelling stories and provides a useful foundation for constructing great questions. In a slightly different vein, understanding your team's strengths opens the door for conversations for possibility about what you can accomplish together by blending strengths. It also helps you argue better by knowing whose assessments to trust on which topics and how to best encourage them to ground their assessments.

ORGANIZATIONAL STRATEGIES

Most people think of a strategy as a ploy or plan for the future. And it certainly can be that. But a strategy can also be a pattern of past actions—not what was intended, but what resulted. Henry Mintzberg calls this an *emergent strategy*. "Strategies," he says, "form as well as are formulated. So even good ones need not necessarily be conscious and purposeful."[29]

A classic example of emergent strategy was Honda's entry into the United States motorcycle market. The Boston Consulting Group, in a case study used for years in MBA classes, described this as a deliberate market strategy conceived by Honda's senior executives in Japan. Most businesspeople believed this story because it matched the way they thought about strategy: as a plan for the future. Then Richard Pascale stepped in. When he interviewed the Honda managers who sold the first motorcycles in Los Angeles, a dramatically different story surfaced. Their assignment was to sell large motorcycles that company executives assumed would appeal to American consumers (because Americans "like big vehicles"). But this didn't work out as planned. What happened instead is that people in Los Angeles started calling Sears to request smaller Honda motorcycles that weren't even on sale in the United States. Why? Because they saw Honda salesmen driving around Los Angeles on these smaller vehicles. Over time, the sales managers caught onto what was happening—they noticed a pattern of behavior—and responded by placing orders for the smaller motorcycle. In Mintzberg's words, the company's strategy wasn't formulated. It formed.[30]

Another example of emergent strategy was Intel's decision to exit the memory business. There is a famous story about how, at a pivotal moment, Gordon Moore and Andy Grove conducted a thought experiment in which they fired themselves, physically left the room, came back in, and decided to stop manufacturing the DRAM (Dynamic Random Access Memory), which was Intel's bread-and-butter product. This story is true, and it presents a wonderful illustration of possibility leadership. Humility and courage meshed in a single moment, bringing a powerful question, great listening, a conversation for possibility, and two leaders turning toward one another.

Yet there is a story behind this story. You can find it described in Grove's book, *Only the Paranoid Survive,* and detailed in Robert Burgelman's book-length study of Intel, *Strategy is Destiny.* A few years before the famous thought experiment, Intel middle managers had started shifting production away from memory and toward other products like microprocessors. They had seen what Moore and Grove had not: the market and field of competition were shifting. As importantly, they were able to translate this heretical insight into action without senior management approval. Why? Because microprocessors produced higher margins than DRAM. They automatically received favorable treatment in decisions about manufacturing allocation.

Grove and Moore's thought experiment was therefore more than simply a deliberate strategy. It was also a ratification of a pattern of behavior that had occurred for years. It recognized an emergent strategy and gave it a large stamp of approval.

There are countless other examples of emergent strategy— Mintzberg's writings are full of them—yet the world of management continues to assume that strategy is always a plan you design rather than a pattern you discover. The reasons for this range from the cultural (deliberate strategies give us a sense of control and constancy) to the pedagogical (deliberate strategies are easier to study and explain) to the political (if strategies emerge, then who needs CEOs?) to the financial (without deliberate strategies to sell, how will blue chip consulting firms stay in business?). There is no getting around it: deliberate strategy is here to stay.

But let's give emergent strategy its rightful place. That means building the capacity within yourself and your organization to recognize patterns of behavior that just might, from the proper vantage point, reveal something significant: New customers and markets to capture; competition that is greater or less than you assumed; and businesses to enter, grow, diminish, or exit. Just consider the possibilities. In fact, you may even discover new ways of tapping into and combining the gifts of your people as their own strengths rise into view.

STRENGTHS OF PEOPLE

People surprise you. Just when you think you know who they are and what they are capable of, they do something completely unexpected. Like lead a seemingly unmanageable team, resolve an insurmountable human conflict, or shine in an area everyone "just knows" they are weak. This is the limitation of putting people in boxes as though they are inanimate objects. This is also the reason we speak about "human potential" and, in honest moments, acknowledge that each person's true potential is a mystery.

Fortunately, as a manager, there is something you can do: watch your team members very, very closely. Notice what activities are easy and effortless for them. Notice what allows them to enter a state of "flow," when they are so immersed in action that they lose track of space and time. Notice, too, what gets them out of bed in the morning and what keeps them up at night (which, if you watch closely, are different things). Notice how they behave around you versus how they behave around others. Notice what they're like in the morning as compared to the afternoon, what gets them emotionally triggered versus what relaxes them, and what they do when they don't know what to do.

When you observe like this and when you do it with care, you'll pick up on patterns. These patterns will inform the decisions you make, like what assignments to give them, which teammates to match them with, how to help them build their careers, and what it takes to keep them engaged, happy, and employed in your organization. These decisions, in turn, will shape the possibilities you create as a manager and the mood you evoke in the organization around you.

This ability to see patterns in people is a powerful gift. If your organization has solid practices for succession planning and leadership development, you can put that gift to use there. Because now you are a talent scout. Your job is to assess different people's performance and potential and to discern where to invest the organization's development resources—not training or coursework, but the time and attention of senior managers. Notice the patterns of behavior you see in people two and three levels below you in the organization. What challenges do they face in their on-the-job experiences? What are they learning from these experiences? When they move to different roles or assignments, how do they handle the transitions? What do new challenges reveal about their capacity to rise to the highest levels? And, to make things real, how does it feel when you are around them? Do you feel a sense of constraint and resignation, or are you energized by a feeling of possibility? Can you allow yourself to be emotionally affected by others even while you try to evoke positive emotions in them? Can you become part of the very pattern that you are seeing?

PATTERN RECOGNITION

The good stuff doesn't always come naturally, particularly when nobody has taught it to you. Discovering emergent strategies and recognizing strengths in people are both acts of pattern recognition. They involve not analysis, breaking a whole down into its parts, but synthesis, bringing the parts together into a whole. Almost nobody teaches synthesis—anywhere. If your schooling was like mine, you learned to analyze, not synthesize, and took pride in being "analytical." (My organic chemistry and macroeconomics textbooks didn't teach synthesis). Instructors specialized in particular subjects—whether mathematics, French, mechanical engineering, or political science—and rarely strayed from them. In high school, I took a marvelous class that integrated

American History and English (titled "Integrated"), but that was a big exception. Within any given class, when it came time to integrate all that you had learned during the year, was this an exciting moment of synthesizing the myriad lessons into a cohesive whole? Hardly. It was a time to stress out, eat poorly, sleep little, and hold your breath until it was over.

Most organizations don't do much better at teaching you to recognize patterns or synthesize. They're divided into departments or functions, each with its own language and rules. If you're an individual contributor and you propose something bold that connects your work to another function or department, you may get patted on the back, but it's equally likely that you will be discouraged from pursuing such a collaboration because it's "outside your scope." If, on the other hand, you're a first line manager, your scope is larger, but in most places you're still rewarded for the success of your team, rather than the success of the larger organization. As you rise to higher levels in the organization, you take on greater scopes of responsibility that require you to see and integrate more and more perspectives. To paraphrase educator Robert Kegan, every promotion brings new "mental demands," the challenge to handle ever greater complexity.

Challenge is essential to growth and, the research tells us, pivotal to leadership development. But it creates distress and disorientation rather than development when not joined by sufficient support. As the complexity in your job rises, who teaches you how to manage this complexity? Who models how to synthesize and make sense of all the perspectives that suddenly confront you? If you are among the fortunate few, your organization has a long tradition of helping managers learn how to stretch their minds to meet each successive growth in scope. That responsibility is owned by your current boss, who not only interacts with you regularly (unlike a mentor or external coach), but also has gone through that very leadership passage herself. She can teach you because she has lived it herself.

Wouldn't that be nice?

I ask the question because it's likely you're not one of the fortunate ones in this situation. Instead, you have to figure everything out for yourself. Your boss either hasn't gone through this leadership passage herself, doesn't have the skill to coach you through it, or simply lacks the time or incentive. She has her mind on other things, and what's the reward for developing people anyhow? If she exposes you to the people and assignments that would teach you what you cannot learn now, she might lose you to another division. There's no victory in that. As a result, the virtue of teaching you to see patterns and synthesize takes a back seat to the vice of hoarding talent. Actually, to call it a "vice" is misleading. Your boss is acting in integrity with what the organization expects.

It's a sad story, not just because the missed opportunity is so great, but because what is required to seize it is relatively simple. Seeing patterns is primarily a cognitive act. You do it with your brain. Yes, emotion can support or detract from synthesis. Yes, as we'll soon see, a relaxed and centered body helps. But the core act of synthesis is primarily cognitive. So in a world of managers who have spent years honing their cognitive abilities, this seems like the perfect thing for experienced managers to teach their direct reports. If I didn't know any better, I'd figure that the managerial ranks would be filled with capable synthesizers. But they're not.

Fortunately, as we've seen, every complaint points to a commitment. Once I recognize how much I value synthesizing and join with others who share this commitment, my disappointment morphs into resolve.

And so I ask the same of you. What would it be like to become really good at seeing patterns, say in the strengths of your team? What possibilities would this create for your team's work together? What greater influence would this allow you to have within your organization? Most importantly, what would it feel like to be the kind of leader who was a whiz at spotting others' strengths and knowing how to employ them to good ends?

CHAPTER 17

HEALING YOUR ACHILLES HEEL

DON'T LET YOUR Achilles Heel become an Achilles Hell.

If you're human, you have flaws. And there is probably one big one that can screw up your career or, at the very least, limit your potential for possibility leadership and/or big promotions. We call this the Achilles Heel in homage to a mythical Greek warrior who was invulnerable in battle except for his foot. I describe the Achilles Heel as a set of habits wired into your brain and body that limits your repertoire of leadership behaviors. In other words, it constrains your degrees of freedom. Fortunately, the latest neuroscience teaches us that these habits can be rewired even well into adulthood.[31] The leaders I work with accomplish this through deliberate practice and rigorous self-observation. This takes courage and focus, but the result is greater energy to respond to complex decisions and challenges.

How would you describe your Achilles Heel?

Here's my hunch: you have a very good idea of the behaviors that get you into trouble. One or two dozen performance reviews have taught you that. But do you know what is behind these behaviors? Wouldn't it be nice to have a better understanding of the thought patterns and habitual emotional reactions that produce these behaviors so you can nip those habits in the bud?

No, not really, Amiel. That sounds unpleasant. Pass the beer nuts.

Let's assume you're willing to muster the courage to delve into these inner experiences. Let's say you are up for honing in on what makes you tick—and that you might actually appreciate what you get out of this. How might you learn about your Achilles Heel, and what would you do with the new understanding?

A BRIEF HISTORY OF THE ACHILLES HEEL

Before we go there, I'd like to provide a very brief history of the Achilles Heel concept in leadership. In the late 70s and early 80s, researchers at the Center for Creative Leadership (CCL) identified a set of leadership *derailers*. If you're a train speeding down a track (rather than a Greek warrior entering battle), these are the factors that can throw you off track. It was wonderful research, and it had several significant upshots. One was for organizations to take the time to identify leaders' derailers and then do something about them. At that point in time, leadership derailers generally weren't on organizations' radar. First, because the concept hadn't been invented and, second, because in the United States companies had experienced a remarkable period of growth without significant global competition since World War II. I don't think it's a coincidence that the CCL study happened shortly after the United States stopped being the only economic game in town. A second upshot of the research was that certain organizations saw the value of going beyond the simple reward strategy of promoting managers up the chain.

To teach managers the lessons they needed to lead on a larger level, CCL suggested employing lateral moves. For example, if you have an operations manager with solid results and great potential who is lousy at listening to others, put them in a customer service management role where the job itself forces them to practice listening.

As robust and practical as the CCL's research was, it had far less impact on managerial practice than the researchers had hoped.[32] First, the notion that leaders have a single big potential derailer was far outshined in the marketplace by the concept of competencies. When your organization asks you to do a 360, the result is a report that lists anywhere from fifteen to a hundred different competencies. A bunch are strengths. A bunch are weaknesses (or "development areas" or "opportunity areas"). This is all fine and good, but the sheer number of items detracts from the focus on a single Achilles Heel. When I work with leaders who have received a 360, my first task is to help them find the signal in the midst of all this noise.

The other competition to the notion of Achilles Heel is the growth of the strengths-based school of leadership development. If you've taken the StrengthsFinder instrument, you've been part of this school. Personally, I can't imagine coaching leaders without an understanding of their strengths. And I would agree that leveraging your strengths is a wonderful way to develop. Where the strengths-based school goes overboard, in my opinion, is in its insistence that people develop best in their area of greatest strength. This may be true for many first-line employees, but it is not for managers for the simple reason that the complexity and pressure of their roles is incompatible with an unattended Achilles Heel. Someone gets hurt. So my take—grounded in research and my own experience—is that leaders develop best in *both* their area of greatest strength *and* their Achilles Heel.

For strengths, my favorite instruments are StrengthsFinder 2.0, created by the Gallup Organization, and the VIA Survey of Character Strengths. The latter is available for free by registering on the University of Pennsylvania's Authentic Happiness web site. There are also many excellent books on this topic like *Now, Discover Your Strengths, Strengths-Based Leadership*, and *Go Put Your Strengths to Work*.

IDENTIFYING YOUR ACHILLES HEEL

As for identifying your Achilles Heel, there are a number of instruments and tools you can use. My favorite is one with an unusual name: the Enneagram. It's a model of nine personality types. Each type describes a deep and fundamental pattern of making sense of experience that drives what you pay attention to and what you ignore. Remember the listening filters from the last chapter? Each listening filter is an expression of a particular personality type. As we've seen, if you're not attentive to it, it can get you into all sorts of trouble. That's one reason I joke that the Enneagram describes nine potential paths to Achilles Hell. Fortunately, the Enneagram also shows the nine roads to possibility leadership precisely by helping you get free from the constraints of your Achilles Heel. Rather than putting you in a box, it shows you the box you put yourself in every day—and how to escape it.

The nine Enneagram types are known as The Perfectionist, The Helper, The Achiever, The Individualist, The Investigator, The Loyal Skeptic, The Enthusiast, The Challenger, and the Peacemaker. My favorite books about this topic, *Personality Types* and *The Wisdom of the Enneagram*, both by Don Riso and Russ Hudson, describe how each type has Unhealthy, Average, and Healthy manifestations. In other words, just identifying your type doesn't tell you immediately "how you are." You also need to assess your relative level of health within that type. Most leaders, most organizations, and most families operate at an Average level of health. This means there is a lot of room for growth. To give you a taste of how this works, here are quick-and-dirty summaries of three different Enneagram types that I've lifted from *Personality Types*.

- *Type One: The Reformer.* The key motivation is to be right, have integrity, and be consistent with their ideals. At the highest level of Health they "become extraordinarily wise and discerning...Humane, inspiring, and hopeful. [At an Average level,] dissatisfied with reality, they become high-minded idealists, feeling that it is up to them to improve everything...They point out how things 'ought' to be...Become orderly and well-organized but impersonal, rigid, emotionally constricted...highly critical both of self and others... [At an Unhealthy level they] make very severe judgments of others, while rationalizing their own actions... [They are] condemnatory, punitive and cruel in order to rid themselves of whatever they believe is disturbing them."

- *Type Six: The Loyal Skeptic.* The key motivation is to have safety and security. At the highest level of Health they "become self-affirming, trusting of self and others [which] leads to true courage, positive thinking, leadership, and rich self-expression... [At an Average level they] start investing their time and energy into whatever they believe will be safe and stable...Constantly vigilant, anticipating problems... [They have s]trong self-doubt as well as suspicion about others' motives... [At an Unhealthy level they] become clingingly dependent and self-disparaging with acute inferiority feelings...Feeling persecuted, that others are 'out to get them,' they lash out and act irrationally, bringing about what they fear."

- *Type Nine: The Peacemaker.* The key motivation is to have serenity and peace of mind. At a Healthy level they are "optimistic, reassuring, supportive: have a healing and calming influence—harmonizing groups, bringing people together. A good mediator, synthesizer, and communicator... [At an Average level they] become self-effacing and agreeable, accommodating themselves, idealizing others and 'going along' with things to avoid conflict…Become passive, disengaged, unreflective, and inattentive… [They p]ractice wishful thinking and wait for magical solutions… [At an Unhealthy level they] do not want to deal with problems: become depressed and listless, dissociating self from all conflicts. Neglectful and dangerously irresponsible."[33]

I trust you won't try to identify your type from these brief descriptions. That requires more thorough exploration. Instead, I invite you to notice the wide variation in motivation between just these three types. They are very different! That's the great thing about pinpointing what makes you tick: it suggests very specific practices for becoming a healthier version of your personality type and therefore increasing your odds of practicing possibility leadership.

Another useful tool for working with your Achilles Hell is the Hogan Development Inventory (HDI) which identifies "the dark side of personality—qualities that emerge in times of increased strain and can disrupt relationships, damage reputations, and derail peoples' chances of success."[34] The HDI measures personality along 11 scales like Excitable, Skeptical, Leisurely, and Colorful. One thing I like about the HDI is that it consciously builds upon the Center for Creative Leadership's pioneering research on derailment by making the derailers identifiable.[35]

HEALING YOUR ACHILLES HEEL

What do you do after you've honed in on your Achilles Heel? Both the Enneagram and HDI provide a wealth of answers. Here are my suggestions:

1.   As you consider each outer practice of possibility leadership, ask yourself, *"How might my Achilles Heel get in the way of successfully taking on this practice?"* For example, as someone who identifies with

Type Six (The Loyal Skeptic) on the Enneagram, I find that my pattern of seeing what could go wrong puts me at risk of the following: putting a damper on conversations for possibility by pointing out risks, turning against others when I fear I cannot trust them, getting stuck in complaints, taking my assessments to be the truth, assuming some relationships will never improve, only telling stories that confirm a pessimistic view of the future, getting distracted from listening by worst-case scenario thoughts, and asking mediocre questions because I'm afraid the great ones will blow people away.

2. *Take on new inner practices that elevate you to the healthier levels* of your personality type (in the case of the Enneagram). For me, this includes what Martin Seligman calls *universalizing the positive* and *particularizing the negative.*[36] When something positive happens, like I give a great speech, I have two options: particularize it by telling myself, "I got lucky" or "That was an easy audience" or universalize it by thinking to myself, "I'm a good speaker." Universalizing the positive reinforces my sense of competence and confidence and therefore erodes negative thinking. A similar principle applies when something negative happens. Let's say I trip on a flight of stairs. I can universalize this by calling myself "clumsy," or I can particularize this by thinking, "oops, slipped, no biggie." Particularizing the negative reinforces my resilience and builds a sense of myself as capable.

3. *Observe your Achilles Heel in action.* What triggers it? How does it operate? If you do this with candor and humility, you may start calling B.S. on yourself, the subject of the next chapter.

CHAPTER 18

CALLING B.S. ON YOURSELF

KNOWLEDGE OF YOUR Achilles Heel has an additional benefit. It allows you to do unto yourself what you like to do unto others: call B.S.

For those new to this term or from other cultures, that means call bullshit. In polite parlance: point out that someone is full of—and deluding—himself.

Calling B.S. on yourself is an unnatural act. Like many of the other practices in this book, it isn't something you've been taught, nor is it something that comes easily to you. This changes once you develop the habit of recognizing your conditioned patterns of thinking and reacting. Suddenly you start to see what was previously invisible to you: how these patterns distract you from being present. You're there in your body, but not really; how else to explain all those days and nights working through exhaustion? You're there with other people, but not fully; after all, what good is an overactive mind if it can't interfere with your awareness of others' experiences?

A few examples of what might prompt you to call B.S. on yourself. You realize that:

- The instinct to be strong and avoid vulnerability blocks you from seeing all the ways you overpower and intimidate people.
- The urge to know everything blocks your curiosity about what others think and what this reveals about them.
- The obsession with success pushes you to race around people without building a single authentic relationship.
- The preoccupation with worst-case scenarios blinds you to the beauty and joy you could be experiencing at this very moment
- The pressure to be correct about everything twists your body into a stiff pretzel that cannot relax much less enjoy all the fun stuff happening around you

Every time you catch yourself in such a pattern, you stop and wonder *What the hell is going on here? And, incidentally, who is running this show?*

Over time, it becomes increasingly difficult to make the case that somebody else is to blame. Like a compact fluorescent light bulb that takes a second to illuminate after the switch has been flipped, your mind eventually has an odd realization: the person running this show is you. It's not the best version of you. It's not you expressing your highest potential. Instead, it's the currently available version, the one calling the shots most of the time.

At this moment, as the light of awareness brightens, a voice deep within you rises from the depths of your being and calls out in a forceful yet loving tone:

Bullshit!

You smile. Who ever thought you'd be calling B.S. on yourself?

As my late grandmother, Thelma, would often say in her New York Jewish accent, "In a million years, who ever heard of such a thing?"

Well, there is a first time for everything.

And here's the surprise: calling B.S. on yourself fills you with energy and a feeling of great possibility. Not because it's pleasant to finally name the weird things you do, but because the person who is naming this weirdness is a deeper and better version of yourself. This is the truth-seeking better angel of your nature. This is the one who can rise to the challenge of possibility leadership.

CHAPTER 19

MANAGING COMMITMENTS

THIS BOOK DOESN'T contain a chapter about managing time because I don't know how to manage time. The clock proceeds at the same pace no matter what I'm doing. But I do have something to say about managing commitments, specifically commitments to yourself.

Declaring a new possibility for yourself or your organization is huge. It opens new avenues, particularly when combined with many of the other practices I've described. But what happens to everything you were doing before you declared a new possibility and before you decided to take on new practices? It would be nice to think that all of the old stuff just vanishes—Poof!—but you know better. This stuff hangs around as calendar items, projects, activities, and action items. It's just like those three boxes of cookies you bought before you decided to cut down on the sugar. They're still in the cupboard, and if nothing else changes, you're bound to open them up and munch on a few tasty treats as you are accustomed to doing.

Managing commitments to yourself is the meat and potatoes of possibility leadership. It's the domain in which you make choices about what to stop doing, what to start doing, and how to makes these shifts without overloading yourself, underloading yourself, or staying up all night.

This topic is key in two overlapping areas:

1. Managing your calendar.
2. Designing and using a trusted system (including but going way beyond your calendar) for managing everything that matters to you.

MANAGING YOUR CALENDAR

One way to manage commitments is through the calendar. This activity invites more excuses, rationalizations, and white lies than just about any other I've encountered. I see this happening often with people trying to take on the practices of possibility leadership. A few examples:

*   A senior executive tells me he'd like to hire me as a coach but is "too busy right now." A year later he hires me. We work really well together. He rises to my challenge and gratefully accepts my support. He actually starts to speak, listen, and think differently. This produces a demonstrably positive impact on his team. However, it's not enough. He doesn't mend all the bridges that have needed mending, so his detractors eventually pull him down. He gets asked to leave the company. "I wish I had started working with you a year earlier," he laments. I can't bring myself to remind him that this is precisely how long he postponed the start of our work. Two questions linger in my mind. First, what exactly was he so busy doing that he ignored the actions most critical to his own career success? Second, why didn't he adjust his calendar to reflect these priorities?

- I'm helping a middle manager prepare for a big presentation. As the date gets closer, it becomes clear to me that she's not giving the project the time and attention it deserves. I finally challenge her to take a hard look at her calendar. "It's time," I say, "to shift the burden of proof onto each event on your calendar: is this essential to do now? If not, cancel it or reschedule." She cancels 75% of her events over the next week. The presentation turns out reasonably well—not as well as if she had done this earlier but much better than if she had kept her calendar intact.

- An executive tells his coach that he has no time on his calendar next week for scheduling important conversations that the coach has assigned as a practice. A half hour later, while working with the executive's assistant to schedule coaching meetings, the coach discovers that the next week's calendar contains many free blocks of time. What is going on here? Amnesia? Deceit? Either way, it's fair to assume that the reason the executive is refusing to schedule those conversations isn't because of time, but because he expects the conversations to be uncomfortable.

Like budgets and bank statements, calendars reveal what's important to you. If something you value is not on your calendar, one of two things is true: either you're managing it from a checklist of some sort or you're simply not doing it. That's the genius of having someone look at your calendar with a curious eye. In the words of Chris Argyris, it shows you not your espoused theory of what you care about, but your "theory-in-use," the one that's actually functioning every day.[37]

Comparing the contents of your calendar to your commitments is not the same thing as changing your calendar to reflect these commitments. However, it is a monumental leap forward. As you become aware of how poorly your calendar reflects your commitments—which is a common phenomenon—a new possibility presents itself. You can take charge of your calendar. As with your complaints and your Achilles Heel, instead of it owning you, you can begin to own it.

When somebody I coach first catches sight of this possibility, there is one thing I consistently do: get her assistant involved. Although I'm happy to take a quick look at the calendar as part of scheduled coaching meetings, the assistant's job is to manage that calendar every day. The first thing we do is get aligned about the current state of the calendar and how to improve it. (*Wouldn't it be nice if____?*) Then, I encourage the executive and her assistant to make this priority-setting an ongoing part of their calendar discussions.

I once had an idea for improving the return on investment from executive development. Don't just get a bunch of high potential leaders together. Include their assistants part of the time. Give these pivotal people an opportunity to be with their managers not just in executing on powerful "aha" experiences, but also while actually having those experiences. Let the assistants witness the power of these insights and get a tangible sense of how hard it is to act on them. In reality, many assistants are more aware of these matters than their bosses, so think of this activity as a way to fully enroll them in their bosses' new commitments. That way, they are even more likely to stand firm about tough calendar decisions when their bosses waver. After all, in the kingdom of calendaring, the assistant is queen (or king).

DESIGNING AND USING A TRUSTED SYSTEM

Many commitments don't appear on a calendar. They show up in a variety of systems for tracking activities, projects, promises, and actions. The most common albeit least sophisticated system is a "To Do" list coupled with the manager's memory. Do you remember the first time you created a To Do list? Mine had to do with mowing the lawn. Do you use one now? If so, how would you describe the results it is giving you?

For many years, I took great pride in my To Do list. Having it and using it meant that I was an organized person. Plus it helped me remember to do things. The only problem was that it didn't actually work that well. Before the age of PDAs and smart phones, I had to remember to carry it around with me. Even after technology changed, the more successful I was at keeping the list accurate, the harder it became to find the things I could actually do in that place at that time. Too many items to sort through! In addition, it was hard to track things that other people had promised to me. Where do those go on a To Do list? Finally, putting stars next to things that were important and/or urgent didn't help me decide what to do when the amount of time I had was insufficient for the task. Although I didn't admit it for many years, the To Do list wasn't serving me anywhere near as much as I needed it to.

Then one day my friend Michael Dolan called me up to say he had accepted a job with the David Allen Company. I had heard the name and remembered seeing Allen's book, *Getting Things Done*, on the shelf. But I'd never actually opened it.

I like to understand what my friends are doing, particularly when it's roughly related to my own work. This seemed to fit the bill, particularly when I noticed the book's subtitle, *The Art of Stress-Free Productivity*. There was no doubt in my mind I could become more productive, and I'm always open to ways to reduce stress. So I read the book.

A good decision!

I quickly learned that Getting Things Done (known widely as GTD) has two important virtues: it's powerful, and it's practical. The heart of GTD is creating a trusted system for identifying what matters to you, translating these things into projects and "next physical actions," and taking action on them.[38] I encourage you to look at the book or David Allen's web site. What you will find is a nifty system that:

- *Clears the mind* of concerns, questions, actions, and projects by providing a trusted system for storing this information. Sometimes I like to joke that GTD is better at clearing the mind than meditation. The two together are like Jordan and Pippen:

unstoppable. Personally, I use a GTD-friendly application called Evernote that works seamlessly with my Mac and iPhone.

- Invites you to distinguish *actionable* items from non-actionable items. Not everything on your mind actually has to happen! The best way to determine this is to ask, "Is this actionable?"[39]

- Provides specific guidance on how to store non-actionable items that are worth keeping. My physical *reference system* improved dramatically when I started organizing all of my physical files in alphabetical order and labeling them with high quality printed labels. My electronic reference system became much easier to use when I stopped creating 24-layer nests of folders and files and chose instead to label files with the subject heading followed by a hyphen and the topic name. For example: Clients—Ernst & Young/Jane Smith—Contract0908 rather than Clients/Ernst & Young/Jane Smith/Contracts/Sept08. Two layers of hierarchy instead of four means fewer clicks of the mouse, i.e. less time spent on a non-value-added activity.

- Encourages you to translate murky ideas and concerns into *next physical actions*—tangible steps you will take—and "desired outcomes" for multi-step projects. For example, if your mind is preoccupied with thoughts about a report you recently wrote, you'll type or write "XYZ Report Checkup" in the Inbox. Later, you may identify a next action as "Email Tabitha about distribution of XYZ report." Or, alternatively, you'll realize it's a multi-step project and call it "Final draft of report distributed to entire team." Then you can list the next action needed to produce this outcome and others that come to mind.

- Reminds you that you don't have to undertake every physical action yourself. Your other options are to *delegate* it to another person or *defer* it to a later time using your calendar or a tickler system of reminders.

- Forces you to categorize and sort physical actions by *context* like "Home," "Errands," "Phone," and "Office." That way, when you're in the car, you can take a quick look at the Errands list and not get distracted by everything else. When you're at home, you can easily see what needs to be done there.

- Gives you a way of tracking commitments others have made to you (the *Waiting For* list) and stuff that interests you but isn't a current commitment (the *Someday Maybe* list, which also could be called the *Guilt Removal List.*)

- Challenges you to keep your trusted system up to date by holding *Weekly Reviews, Dumpster Days* (when you purge your desk, files and cabinets—a very energizing act!), and regular mind dumps in which you clear your thoughts by entering them into your GTD system.

Everyone I know who has tried GTD has enjoyed it, and many swear by it. Lately, I've been considering making it a required part of every coaching program. However, it's not uncommon for managers to start using GTD but not sustain it. Older habits of managing commitments—or avoiding them—return. The To Do list strikes back. Managers love how GTD works but see it as a burden, even though it relieves more burden than it generates. Most importantly, they say they'd love to continue this system, but it takes energy, and they're just too darn tired.

What do you say to someone who cannot manage their system of managing commitments because they're exhausted? "My friend, it's time to manage your physical energy!" This is the topic of the next chapter.

CHAPTER 20

MANAGING PHYSICAL ENERGY

"IF ONE THING is evident about the hectic pace, the orientation to action, the variety and fragmentation of activities of managing, it is the enormous amount of energy that effective managers bring to their work. This is no job for the lazy."

—Henry Mintzberg, *Managing*[40]

Managing may not be a job for the lazy, but it's also not a job for people who are exhausted. Sound like you? If so, it's likely that nowhere in your management education were you taught (a) how much your performance depends upon creating and sustaining physical energy or (b) what enhances your physical energy and what depletes it.

There is a simple reason why you never learned this from mentors, managers, classes, and books: talking about physical energy entails focusing on the body, and nearly every recognized theory of management says not a word about the body. Not a single word.

I find this more than slightly insane.

We can do better. This is why as a coach I start most client meetings by doing a leadership vital signs check. I ask people questions that I'm being paid too much money to ask but that, if unasked, will interfere with the success of coaching: *How's your physical energy level today? How many hours of sleep have you been getting? How many days have you exercised in the past week? What have you been eating lately?*

I'm not embarrassed to ask these questions, but I do like to explain why they matter: "Ching, as you know, the reason we're spending time on this is that if you have no physical energy, everything else we do together will be a waste." I really believe this—and I've seen it come true. One day I'm providing great coaching to a leader, but he's not getting anything out of it because he's wiped out. So I give him a practice related to sleep. Two weeks later, my coaching hasn't improved one iota, nor has the challenge before him shrunk, yet he is suddenly thriving. What's up with that? He's refueled.

Do you remember the last time you felt absolutely energized? Maybe it was this morning. Or maybe it was months ago. Whatever the case, I'd like to help you rebuild your physical energy so that it supports you in practicing possibility leadership—and, frankly, so that you feel more alive, which has value unto itself. I'll do that by describing four dimensions of physical energy: sleep, exercise, nutrition, and renewal.

SLEEP

"Like a drunk, a person who is sleep-deprived has no idea how functionally impaired he or she truly is."
—Charles Czeisler, Harvard Medical School[41]

According to the National Sleep Foundation, 95 percent of us need 7-8 hours per night. Think you need only 5? Maybe you are superhuman. However, research shows that superhuman performers in many fields get *more* sleep than everyone else. A more likely explanation is that you are deceiving yourself. Has it been so long since you got a good night's sleep that you forgot how it actually feels to be fully rested?

I've never been an outstanding sleeper. In fact, it takes concerted effort for me just to sleep adequately. As a result, I've invested a fair amount of time learning about what keeps me from sleeping well and how to remedy the situation. A couple of years ago, I went so far as to purchase a nighttime sleep monitor called the Zeo. Every night for two months, I went to bed wearing a wireless, sensor-equipped headband that tracked how long it took me to fall asleep, how many times I woke up each night (including tiny awakenings I never noticed), and how much I got of each type of sleep (light, deep, and REM). At the end of the measurement period, it was clear that I was sleeping less and waking up more than I had assumed. So I started hunting for understandings of why I wasn't sleeping any better and what to do about it. Here are a few things I learned:

- Getting to sleep and staying asleep are both important, because *uninterrupted sleep* allows the body to rejuvenate and the mind to learn. Let's say you average eight hours per night but wake up three times with an overactive mind and once to use the restroom. In the morning, your body will not feel rested, and your brain will have missed out on the complex learning that happens during REM sleep.

- There are specific things you can do to *fall asleep* more easily. One is to stick to a consistent bedtime and precede it with a common bedtime ritual. An effective ritual will exclude work, email, TV, alcohol, caffeine, controversy, and anything that gets you revved up. Also important is the physical environment. Is the place you sleep quiet and dark? Do your mattress and pillow meet your needs? Small things like these can make a big difference.

- There are other specific things you can do to *return to sleep* quickly when you wake up. If your mind is filled with thoughts, write them down. Take thirty seconds to stretch your back, shoulders and legs. Learn one of the thousands of simple techniques for relaxing your body. One of my personal favorites is tensing and then relaxing every muscle in my body, starting in the head and moving down the body to the feet.

- *Sleep loss is cumulative.* If you only sleep five hours per night for a week, one night of sleeping ten hours isn't going to cut it. Your cumulative sleep deficit is 21 hours (three hours per night for seven nights), so it will take more than ten ten-hour sleep nights to catch up.

- *Power naps* make a difference. Fifteen years ago, I read that Bill Clinton started to power nap when he learned that his hero, JFK, took power naps—and JFK learned this from his hero, Winston Churchill. That very afternoon, I took my first 20-minute power nap. Actually, it was a 40-minute activity: 20 minutes to fall asleep and 20 minutes of actual nap time. Several months of practice later, I learned to fall asleep in two to three minutes. Now a 20-minute power nap is like grabbing a quick snack between meetings. Fast and effective.

For a full understanding of how you sleep, I recommend *The Promise of Sleep* by the pioneering sleep researcher William Dement. For practical tips on how to fall asleep more easily, surf the web. The Quantified Self movement ("self-knowledge through numbers") is filled with people experimenting with new ways to live a healthy life, including getting quality sleep. As with many of the practices I've introduced, try out a bunch of stuff and watch closely to see what works for you.

EXERCISE

Like many kids my age, growing up meant running around outside and playing a lot of sports. My favorite sport—and my first love in life— was soccer. I started playing in fourth grade when a new kid in town dropped a black-and-white ball on the grass and started kicking it around. *That's a strange looking kickball,* I thought to myself. So I asked him, "What is that?" "A soccer ball," he replied. "Come, and I'll show you how to play." Before I knew it, I had completely lost interest in kickball and was playing pickup soccer games every day after school until dark. The boy who showed me how to play, Seth, was an excellent player, and he introduced me to many other good players. After three hours of soccer every day for a few months, I got pretty good. By the end of the year, when the city held its annual "travel league" tryouts, I received the second highest score among a few hundred kids.

Something else happened, too. I got in really good shape. Keeping up with Seth and the other players hour after hour built muscles and stamina. And once I started playing on a competitive team that practiced regularly, I got in even better shape. It was wonderful, particularly since getting conditioned wasn't the purpose of soccer. It was a by-product. The purpose was to have fun and to win (not always in that order).

What does this make you think of in your own life? Have you ever had the experience of getting in great shape doing something you love rather than purely to get in shape?

If you're like me, it may have been awhile. I have friends and colleagues who continue to play competitive sports into their 40s and 50s, but they are an exception. Most people I know get in shape by *trying* to get in shape. Lifting weights, going out for a run, or getting on the Stairmaster can provide intrinsic fulfillment, but only if you approach these exercises in a very particular way. For most people, working out for the sake of working out often feels more like a chore. Sure, it feels great *after* you are finished, but the activity itself can feel dull and/or painful.

Does this sound familiar? Wouldn't it be nice if getting in shape felt engaging or at least less arduous?

I find it helpful to answer each question separately: first, if it were possible to make working out more joyful and engaging, how would you do this? Second, if your goal were, more modestly, simply to stay in shape regardless of how fun the experience is, how might you do that?

Here are ideas for making exercise more engaging:

- *Do something you have always loved doing* but perhaps haven't done much lately. Is it soccer or tennis? Perhaps racquetball or basketball? Swimming? Or maybe going out dancing? (This very evening, my wife and I are going out for high-energy dancing at a club that caters to the over-40 crowd).

- *Try something new that looks fun.* Recently, my friend, Jordan Gruber, introduced me to rebounding, which he describes as "bouncing up and down on a high-quality rebounder or mini-trampoline."[42] For seven years he has bounced while listening to music and even lifting hand weights. I mention this not because this is a fit for you but to open your mind to new possibilities.

- *Focus fully on the activity itself.* For many years I would read or watch TV while riding the Elliptical machine or stationary bike. The idea was to "pass the time." One day I realized that the time was certainly passing, but I was missing what was happening. Rather than being "in my body," I was somewhere else. So I switched to what some call mindful workouts. While I'm lifting weights (my primary physical practice these days), my attention is devoted to two things: the movement and my breath. That's it. In between sets or circuits, I like to pause for 60 seconds to take deep breaths and let go of the tension that has built up in my body. Sometimes my body gets so relaxed and present that I actually feel the warmth of the air and hear the sounds of passing cars or the leaves outside rustling in the wind. These are moments of feeling fully alive. Just think of it: pumping iron and meditating at the same time. Who would've thought?

These are a few ideas for making "getting fit" more engaging. I encourage you to try them, discover others, and invent your own. My hunch is you'll find one that creates this new possibility for you.

But what if it doesn't? That brings us to Plan B. Let's assume for the moment that getting fit will never be any more fun or engaging than it is today. How can you ensure that it happens regularly so you get the physical, emotional, and psychological benefits you need to practice possibility leadership?

Here are several insights that have produced significant shifts in the leaders I coach:

- *A short workout is better than no workout.* OK, so your ideal workout length is 60 minutes. Great. If you only have 20 minutes, are you going to excuse yourself for the day, or are you going to ask, *What can I do in 20 minutes?*

- *Aerobic training* is better than no training, but *anaerobic training* (that draws on lactic acid, not oxygen) is at least as useful. If you run or use an Elliptical machine, switch from a long continuous pace to interval training (short bursts of intense activity following by rest). You'll burn more fat and do it in less time. Better yet, consider resistance training using weights.

- *Physically getting into workout clothes* dramatically increases the odds you'll actually work out. It's another great Jedi Mind Trick. Give it a try.

- *Don't depend on a single location.* If your gym is 20 minutes away, don't make your gym the only place you work out. Get equipment at home. See what's available at your workplace. Or create a workout that requires no equipment whatsoever.

- *Get a workout buddy.* I prefer training alone, but many others find it helpful to go to the gym or go out for a run with a close friend or possibly someone who is exclusively a workout buddy.

NUTRITION

Our scientific understanding of nutrition has evolved dramatically over the past two decades. If you're still eating what you ate in the mid 1990s, you're probably not giving your body enough sustained energy and may be building up unnecessary body fat. Until a few years ago, I thought that a "low fat" diet was key, until I learned the difference between healthy and unhealthy dietary fats and realized how quickly sugar and other "fast carbs" convert to body fat.

Here are a few other lessons I've learned:

- *Anything that causes your body's energy to spike and then crash* is worthy of your attention. This includes obvious culprits like caffeine and sugar. It also includes more subtle villains like "fast carbs": carbohydrates that quickly break down into simple sugars and elevate blood glucose levels. One example: white potatoes, which are a complex carb *and* fast. What matters most for blood sugar level is not the complexity of the carb but whether it is fast like white potatoes and white rice or slow like broccoli, spinach, and brown rice.

- *Junk food that makes you feel lousy afterwards*—take a look at that, too. What makes this difficult is that it's possible you are so out of touch with your body sensations that you don't notice. For example, I once loved dipping french fries into a Wendy's Frosty.

What a combination! I knew it wasn't good for me, but, boy, did it taste good. Then one day I actually paid attention to the experience. Here is what I found. Anticipating the treat was great. The first few bites were amazing. The next few bites, a little less so. By the time I got to the bottom of the Frosty cup, the experience was just OK. Thirty minutes later, little aches and discomforts appeared in my body. Yummy switched to Yucky just like that.

- *Eat to create the emotional experience you want* in two hours rather than to resolve the emotions you feel now. Anyone who has tried to lose weight quickly learns that when they're feeling sad, anxious or angry, food can become a way to "fix" the pain. The purpose is to get out of whatever it is you are currently feeling. A radically different approach is to consider not what you want to escape but what you want to create.[43] How would you like to feel in two hours so you can work and live at your best? What foods will support you in having this feeling? Hint: it's probably not french fries and a Frosty.

- *Remember the difference between dietary fat and body fat.* We need a lot of dietary fat and can eat a lot of it (the "good" kind) without increasing our body fat. In contrast, body fat is something many of us want to reduce. In 2011, I was shocked to learn that my body fat was 24.5 percent. Most of it was "organ" fat and therefore invisible to others. My body produced it because for years my diet was low in fat but high in fast carbs.

- *Remember, too, the distinction between healthy and unhealthy dietary fats.* The good kind includes the monounsaturated fats in olive oil and most nuts and the polyunsaturated fats in fatty fish like salmon and tuna. Omega 3s, a polyunsaturated fatty acid, are particularly good for you.

- Don't buy food marketed as "low fat" or "gluten-free" without *looking at the other ingredients.* Odds are good that the food is filled with processed sugar that can quickly end up as body fat.

- *Eat foods that taste good and are good for you.* Take a look at anything Jonny Bowden has written. I like *The 150 Healthiest Foods on Earth.* This book convinced me to eat a lot of avocados—great taste and a healthy fat. Consider other approaches like the Paleo Diet.

- *Watch how much you eat.* Two reasons: (1) too much of even relatively healthy food can leave you sluggish and (2) research shows you probably eat more than you think. As I searched for ways to eat less, I ran across Dan Buettner's book *Blue Zones.* Buettner takes a close look at why some regions of the world like Okinawa and Sardinia have an unusually large percentage of centenarians (people over 100 years old). One practice shared by many is that they eat less. Some use smaller plates. Others eat until they are no longer hungry, rather than until they're full. The Okinawans set an intention before the meal to practice "Hara hachi bi," or stop eating when their stomachs are 80 percent full.[44] Personally, I come from a family where people always ask, "Have you had enough to eat?" The implication of this question: Eat more! Piggybacking off of the Okinawan practice, I prefer to be asked, "Have you hit the 80 percent mark yet?"

RENEWAL

"Periodization refers to the way athletes train in cycles—alternating intense work with periods of recovery daily, weekly, yearly—in an effort to marshall the highest energy for key competitive events. We believe leaders and their teams need to think in similar terms."[45]

—Tony Schwartz, *Be Excellent at Anything*

In our discussion of managing your calendar, we left out one important piece: creating time for renewal. The research shows that peak performers in sports and the performing arts make conscious and calculated use of renewal periods. They only train or work a certain amount each day. Anything more than that taxes their bodies. They alternate periods of intensity with periods of down-time over the course of a week. They also give themselves extended breaks over the course of a year. Recently, I heard an Olympic alpine skier describe a big difference between herself and her teammate, Picabo Street. This skier trained harder for longer, but Picabo took more breaks. Picabo won the medals.

In his outstanding book, *Be Excellent at Anything*, Tony Schwartz lays out the research case for renewal. He advocates for "setting a new rhythm" in organizations, one that embraces renewal as a business necessity and measures what employees produce rather than how long they work.[46] This aligns well with the idea that organizations give people more flexibility with their time as an expression of trust and as a bottom line imperative. Schwartz takes it a step further by proposing that organizations actively encourage people to periodically pause from intense activity to take breaks. His success helping major companies like Sony put these ideas into practice is a testimony to the value of renewal. I'd go so far as to say that possibility leadership itself depends upon people getting enough down-time so they have the physical energy to discover new possibilities and bring them to fruition.

Drawing upon Schwartz's recommendations and my clients' experiences, I offer the following tips for renewing yourself:

- *Take a break every 90 minutes.* This is the longest period of intense activity that our bodies can tolerate before we diminish our reserves. At the very minimum, get up out of your chair, go for a walk, and have a glass of water. Even better, take what my colleague Sean Casey LeClaire calls a "body-centered break." His web site[47] includes several 2-minute guided breaks that will clear your mind and relax your body. Alternatively, there are a number of good apps for concentrated breathing exercises and many basic yoga and stretching practices that can shift your energy and emotional state in minutes.

* *Don't multitask.* Multitasking is a misnomer. In reality, when you're doing three things "at once," you're doing a little of one, then a little of the other. Some call this micro-tasking. It may sound impressive, but it drains attention and energy. Rather than simply bash multitasking, I've invented an alternative that I call *uni-tasking for multiple purposes.* Let me give you a personal example. One day I was reading a book to my three-year-old son and thought to myself, *This is taking a lot of time. I could be practicing that speech I'm going to give.* I started to feel frustration. Then I realized my mind had created a false choice between practicing my speech and reading to my son. Wouldn't it be nice if I could do both at the same time? It seemed like a crazy idea until I remembered that half of speech practice involves volume, tone, and body gestures. All of these things are part of reading children's books; they're unavoidable. So I decided to use the experience of reading to my son to practice shifting my volume, tone, and gestures. At first he looked at me and said, "Daddy, what the heck is that? Read normal!" Soon, he accepted this as one of his father's many idiosyncrasies, and reading to him hasn't been the same since. Uni-tasking for multiple purposes! Wouldn't it be great to find ways to do this at work?

What's the one thing you can do to increase your physical energy? Is it turning off the laptop an hour before bedtime? Or is it eating less and better food for dinner?

Whatever it is, start doing that today.

CHAPTER 21

POSTURING

POSTURING, ACCORDING TO the dictionary, means "trying to impress or mislead others." That doesn't sound like a promising route to possibility leadership. When I speak of posturing, I mean something very different. Here is my personal definition:

Posturing (Verb): Adjusting your body posture to evoke possibility in yourself and others

This new definition is both familiar and strange. The part about adjusting your body to affect others sounds like our old friend, body language. If you cross your arms, people interpret this to mean that you are closed to their ideas. If you scrunch your nose a certain way, they sense you are feeling disgust toward their thoughts and/or toward them (which is often hard to differentiate). In contrast, an open posture and a warm, relaxed facial expression convey to people that you are curious and interested, or at least open and receptive.

This part of Posturing, whether used to positive or negative effect, concerns the impact your body has on others. This is an important topic. For a fun and informative read, I recommend *The Definitive Book on Body Language* by Allan and Barbara Pease. To learn more about the face and what it conveys, the go to person is Paul Ekman. He's the psychologist behind the TV show *Lie to Me* and author of *Emotions Revealed*. Take a look at his web site, which offers online training on how to identify "micro-expressions" and what they mean.

The second half of Posturing is how your body posture affects you *even when nobody is watching*. How you stand, how you hold your head and shoulders, what shape your arms and neck take—these things have an enormous influence on your leadership. They affect your capacity to undertake any of the outer practices of possibility leadership, like arguing better, turning toward others, or neutralizing enemies.

Here's why: body posture simultaneously reflects and creates a mood (in other words, posture and mood evolve together), and mood influences what's possible in life. Certain postures create positive moods like hope, possibility, and curiosity. Other postures create negative moods like angst, resentment, anger, and resignation. Change your posture, and you can change your mood, or at least increase your odds of doing so.

Try this on for size: cross your arms tightly and hunch your back (unless you have a physical condition that prevents this). Then look up and say, "I'm really excited to be here." Feels awkward, doesn't it? That's because you've put your body in a negative mood while saying something positive. These two parts of yourself are out of alignment. In the real world, this won't happen. What will happen instead in this posture is you'll say something critical and perhaps even destructive, because these words better match the mood your body has evoked.

Now do the opposite: Open your posture by sitting or standing upright, pulling your shoulders back and down, and taking a few deep breaths. Relax your facial muscles and eyes. Say the same thing as before: "I'm really excited to be here." Does that feel easier and more natural? It likely will because your posture now supports the positive mood needed to match your words. You're back in alignment with yourself.

This small experiment suggests that posturing is one of the most fundamental inner practices of possibility leadership. In a hardheaded moment, I'd say this even more strongly: don't waste your time trying to improve your leadership without simultaneously focusing on your body posture.

Here are three simple steps you can take to get a reading on your current posture:

1. Track your body posture during the day by *observing yourself in action*.
2. *Ask a trusted colleague to watch you* in action and give you immediate feedback, the more specific the better.
3. *Ask your assistant to take unannounced photos* of you during the day at your desk. Before you go home, take a look at the photos. What do you see?

Once you have a clear sense of your current postural habits, spend some time exploring what it feels like to mix things up a bit. What if you were to relax your shoulders downward? What is it like to breathe from your belly rather than your chest? Instead of leaning forward, how about being upright? What happens when you have both feet on the floor?

I can't give you specific suggestions about this because I cannot see you. Even if you were standing right in front of me, I would still make the same suggestion: try out a bunch of stuff and see what works. There is only one way to learn whether relaxing your shoulders downward relaxes you into a state where you can listen like a master: by trying it repeatedly and tracking the results. There is only one way to know whether putting both feet on the floor gives you the feeling of grounded support you need to flip complaints into commitments: by trying it. In the end, the practice of posturing is a great arena for self-experimentation.

We've now explored seven inner practices of possibility leadership. Which one will have the most value for you? After you have selected an inner practice to go along with the other practice you consider most valuable, it is time to consider *how* to most effectively take on these practices so that they produce real, sustainable results. This is the subject of Part Four.

PART FOUR

HOW TO PRACTICE

CHAPTER 22

DELIBERATE PRACTICE

IN COMPETITIVE SPORTS, music, and the theatrical arts, performers spend far more time preparing for performances than they do performing. They call this "practice" and they do it for a simple reason: to get better. In many sports, athletes and their coaches devote large chunks of time to reviewing video footage of their performances. In football, some say that watching game film is half of coaching.[48] Why don't athletes, musicians, and performing artists rely solely on performance to get better? Wouldn't this save a lot of time? I can think of two reasons:

1. *Different goals.* The goal of performance is to be your best or to win. The goal of practice is to learn and improve. You can and will learn while performing, but if learning is your emphasis, your performance may plummet. Try practicing your layup when your team is down by three points with two seconds to play. Ever seen what happens to a PGA golfer who takes a mulligan in the

middle of a round to practice his golf swing? Better yet, ever seen a ballet dancer stop mid-performance to repeat a move? These things generally don't happen during performances. They happen during practice.

2. *Logistical hurdles.* Many forms of practice cannot happen within a performance because they don't fit logistically. Consider one way that musicians practice. They break the skill (composition) into its parts, practice each part with intent, and get feedback from a teacher. A cellist who did this while performing would quickly lose her audience. Or consider the chess model of practice. You study situations faced by masters of the skill, decide which moves you would make, and compare your moves to theirs. In an actual game of chess—or golf or basketball—there isn't sufficient time for this. Finally, consider the sports conditioning model of practice. You lift weights, run track intervals, and ride the stationary bike to build underlying muscles and stamina needed to perform at a high level. Carrying a dumbbell onto a soccer field during a game would be awkward and dangerous. That's why we have weight rooms.

Given how much time competitive athletes, musicians, and performing artists spend practicing, you would expect people in organizations to schedule time for practice, too. In fact, you would assume that the highest performing people in the roles with the greatest influence on an organization's success would be practicing the most. Their managers (or Board) would demand it, and their compensation would depend upon it. Surely this is how things work...right?

Not at all. People in 21st century organizations don't practice. They just perform. If they work for nine hours, they perform for nine hours. No practice included. Even the very activities that are supposed to produce learning—training—often contain very little actual hands-on practice. As a result, the manager who wouldn't dare play 18 holes of golf without visiting the driving range cannot imagine rehearsing what she's going to say before setting foot in a pivotal meeting. Weird, isn't it?

Actually, it's quite normal, and that's the point. First the bad news. It's highly likely that:

- You've received little support or direction in your career about practicing leadership of any kind, much less possibility leadership.
- Your manager is neither expecting you to practice nor supportive of it.
- Your organization isn't going to reward you for it—at least directly.
- You don't have the foggiest idea of what practicing leadership would look like.

Now the good news:

- Since nobody else is practicing leadership, you don't have to catch up. In fact, you can get ahead. Perform better by practicing more.
- Most forms of practice don't require extra time. You can do them during your regular work experience and by cutting out wasteful activities.
- I'm about to give you very specific tips about how to practice. You can start using them today.

WHAT IS DELIBERATE PRACTICE?

In *Talent is Overrated*, Fortune magazine senior editor Geoff Colvin describes the ingredients of deliberate practice:

- It is designed specifically to improve performance.
- It can be repeated at high volume.

- The person receives continuous feedback from a teacher or coach.
- It requires intense focus and concentration.
- It may not always be fun.[49]

What are some leadership skills you can deliberately practice? Everything I've introduced you to thus far: holding conversations for possibility, turning toward others, flipping complaints to commitments, arguing better, telling stories, and so on.

According to Colvin, there are two different forms of deliberate practice: *direct practice* and *on-the-job practice*.

Direct Practice

The direct or pure form of practice, according to Colvin, can happen using any of the following four approaches: the music approach, in which you break a skill into its parts and practice the parts; the chess approach, in which you replicate situations faced by masters and compare your choices to theirs; the sports conditioning approach, in which you build underlying muscles needed to master a skill; and the sports simulation approach, in which you create simulations of changing circumstances that require fast responses.

Let's say it's time to learn how to argue better. How might you practice this?

- *Music approach.* First break the skill of arguing into its parts. For example: grounding assessments, asking others to ground their assessments, listening with the intent to understand, asking clarifying questions, framing your assessments with powerful declarations, and inquiring what others think of your assessments. Then pick one or two of these components and practice them over and over—not five times, but fifty or a hundred times. To get better, you have to go for volume. And remember to get feedback from a colleague or coach.

- *Chess approach.* This is harder because leadership masters generally don't leave clear trails of their conversations, and certainly not of their arguments. (In contrast, if the skill is public speaking, that's something you *can* replicate and compare). So improvise. Find someone in your organization who is a master at rigorous debate and watch him in action. Take detailed notes of who said what. Then, in a quiet space on your own or with a partner, repeat their words and gestures. The idea isn't to *become* him (you can only be you) but to experience what speaking like him *evokes* in you. Maybe, with enough repetition, some of the words and gestures will actually start to feel like you.

- *Sports conditioning approach.* This is the most unorthodox model of practice for leaders. What does it mean to get conditioned to argue well? What are the underlying muscles you need in an argument? In my experience, the muscles in leadership that need to be conditioned are particular human qualities. Listening to understand requires curiosity. Making powerful declarations requires courage. Grounding your assessments calls for rigor. How curious, courageous, and rigorous are you today? Whatever your current levels of competence, there are ways to lift them up a notch. For example, if you're open to yoga, the warrior pose is a great way to build courage into your body. The martial art of aikido shows you how to blend with the energy of an attacker in a way that protects you without hurting them. Likewise, there are specific breathing and relaxation practices to build curiosity and mental focusing exercises to build rigor. Finally, all leaders need physical energy, so my suggestions around nutrition, exercise, sleep, and renewal fit the conditioning approach.

- *Sports simulation approach.* Recruit a few family members to simulate a debate. Give them a part to play and lines to say. The debate could be one from work or a live argument you need to have with them anyhow (like where to go for vacation).

On-the-Job Practice

Practicing on-the-job requires not new time but new attention. Your calendar may change a little or a lot. What shifts dramatically is how you show up in these experiences, what you do to prepare for them, and how you learn from them afterwards—through reflecting and getting feedback. Think of these four steps—prepare, act, reflect, and get feedback—as the *on-the-job practice cycle:*

- *Prepare:* what you do before a meeting, speech, email, factory tour, customer visit, negotiation, etc.

- *Act:* the meeting, speech, email, tour, visit, or negotiation itself.

- *Reflect:* what you do afterwards to consider what happened, why and how it happened, and what you can learn from it.

- *Get Feedback:* what you do afterwards to elicit other people's perspectives on what they observed.

If you don't enjoy action, you probably shouldn't be a manager. But if you act 100 percent of the time and never prepare, reflect, or get feedback, you won't be an excellent manager. Competent, but not excellent. And possibility leadership? That will be an even bigger stretch.

This is why it is vital to fully understand the four steps of the on-the-job-practice cycle, the topic of the next chapter.

CHAPTER 23

ON-THE-JOB PRACTICE CYCLE

PREPARING

IN ORGANIZATIONS people prepare before they act, but they don't do it particularly well. The preparation is inconsistent, haphazard, not always focused on the events that matter most, and not often done using skillful means.

The most common form of preparation (other than getting dressed in the morning and drinking coffee) is creating meeting agendas. The value of an agenda is most apparent in its absence: conversations are unfocused. They wander. In fact, they can't even go "off track" because there is no track. In contrast, a clear agenda provides discipline and focus.

But there's a problem with agendas: you probably don't use them consistently. For example, take the simple but important example of development conversations. When you meet with direct reports for a development conversation, do you have an agenda? Who creates it? In many organizations, this responsibility falls to the direct report. After all, "they own their careers." But is this a sole ownership—or do you, as their direct manager, hold some responsibility? Even if this isn't in your formal job description, don't you have an opinion about your direct reports' careers and what's possible for them? If so, wouldn't it make sense to allocate some of the development conversation toward this end?

Now, let's assume you start using meeting agendas with greater focus and consistency. Does this make you fully prepared?

Not if you listen to the stories of leaders who are pros at preparation. For them, the creation of an agenda is necessary but not sufficient for meetings and completely irrelevant for activities that involve more improvisational activity. Complete preparation involves getting your head, heart, and gut ready for whatever is going to happen next. I divide this into three categories: *macro-preparing*, which means considering your overall intention and mood going in; *micro-preparing*, which means defining what success looks like and charting how you plan to get there; and *preparing your body*.

Macro-Preparing

Assume you have a solid practice of managing commitments and therefore are attending the events you most need to attend. Before you set foot in any particular event, take five minutes to ask yourself the following questions:

1. What would you like this event to accomplish? This is not what you want to achieve, but what you want the group to achieve.
2. What can you contribute to achieving this result? What perspective, what questions, what listening, what ideas? Or maybe the value you can add is to invite a new voice to the conversation.
3. What's your general mood around this event? Are you enthusiastic? Resigned? Resentful? Be honest with yourself. It's a

rare manager who doesn't feel resigned or resentful about at least one event on their calendar every day.

4. What assessment is behind this mood? Let's say you feel resigned. Do you think of this group as a waste? Or is it a high-powered group that you assess to be poorly led or heading in a dangerous direction? Perhaps you place a low assessment on your own ability to add value to the group?

5. What can you do to shift yourself into a mood of possibility? Do this.

6. Once you feel more positive, repeat questions 1 and 2 with an emphasis on wondering what is possible.

Ironically, macro-preparing for experiences is more than just an act of preparation. It gives you an opportunity to declare that you care about something and are committed to bringing your best to it. This simple declarative act can do wonders for bringing your full presence to the events on your calendar.

Micro-Preparing

If macro-preparing involves declaring what matters to you and why, micro-preparing involves assessing what success looks like and what strategies you will use to get there. Consider asking yourself these questions:

1. Given your intended contribution, how will you know you've been successful? Is there anyone you can ask for feedback to help you make this assessment?

2. Can you visualize what success looks like? Consider doing a visualization exercise to picture things going well.

3. What approach will you take to make this contribution?

4. What could get in the way? How will you handle these challenges?

5. What can you do at the beginning of the event to ensure you are present, centered, and grounded?

6. How will you practice [insert the leadership skill you most need to develop] in this conversation?

7. Is this meeting important enough that you'd like to rehearse in advance? If so, when and with whom?

Preparing Your Body

The more important the conversation—the higher the stakes and the greater the odds of emotions escalating—the more crucial it is to prepare your body. I find it sad to hear about people who have performed poorly in presentations or meetings because they skipped lunch or forgot to go to the bathroom. To invest so much time, energy, brainpower and heart in an activity and then flub it because you forgot to do something you learned at age five—this is the ultimate preventable bummer.

Preparing your body therefore includes but goes beyond the practices introduced in the chapter on physical energy. Yes, it is useful to get good sleep, get in shape, eat nutritiously, and regularly renew yourself *in general*. It is also helpful for *particular events* on your calendar to ensure that your body is present, centered, and grounded:

*   As you walk into each new room or situation, *take a few long deep breaths*. Feel your feet on the ground. If you're sitting, feel your bottom and back on the seat. Are your legs parallel to the ground? If not, adjust the height of the seat. (A seat at the wrong height affects your posture, and we know what impact that has).

*   *Remind yourself of the possibility* you are committed to. A simple phrase or visual image does the trick. One manager I worked with tells himself *relax* before important meetings, and it works: he relaxes and becomes more open and positive.

- *Notice any tension in your body.* Feel a knot in your shoulders? Imagine your breath going straight to the shoulders. Feel the knot's tightness—and then marvel as it gradually softens.

ACTING

After preparation comes action. The one thing I want to say here: make sure to show up, if for no other reason than to give yourself material for reflection and feedback.

REFLECTING

After acting comes reflecting. The great thing about this part of the on-the-job-practice cycle is that it requires only one person—you—and just a bit of time—5-10 minutes—yet can produce extraordinary learning.

In 1973 Henry Mintzberg did something truly revolutionary for a scholar. Instead of just theorizing about the life of managers, he actually followed a bunch of senior executives as they went about their day and took detailed notes of what he saw. Perhaps his most famous observation from that study was that executives at every level work at an unrelenting pace and are continuously interrupted. As one executive told him, managing is "one damn thing after another."[50]

A downside is that most managers spend a very small amount of time reflecting on what they've done and what it means. The job is never done, the pace is unrelenting, and the interruptions are frequent. When is there time to reflect? That's unfortunate, because reflecting is how we see patterns, make sense of our experience, and learn.

Notice I said that "most" managers reflect little. More accurate would be to say "all but the best" managers. In his study, Mintzberg found that "a remarkable number of effective managers are reflective: they know how to learn from their own experience; they explore numerous options; and they back off when one doesn't work, to try another."[51]

Implicit in this notion of reflection is paying attention without judgment. After all, on any given day managers experience unpleasant surprises, encounter uncomfortable situations, and get emotionally triggered. The purpose of reflection is not to wallow in these experiences—or even to triumph in successes—but instead to notice what happened and make sense of it. This can include:

- Making grounded assessments about why something happened.
- Getting a clearer understanding of people you work with and what makes them tick.
- Mapping your own emotional geography, including the early indicators that you are about to get angry or fearful.
- Gaining new insights about how your team functions or how it fits into the larger organization.
- Recognizing political dynamics and the myriad expressions of power and influence.
- Learning about your company's customers and suppliers.
- Reconsidering something that's been nagging you all day in a way that allows you to be at peace with it and/or take effective action.
- Considering what you will do differently tomorrow, next week, and next month.

The genius of reflection is that it is incredibly simple. All you need is a little time, a little quiet, and a few powerful questions. In fact, the questions don't even need to be that powerful. If you find the time and the space, asking one or two half-decent reflective questions produces far better results than skipping the act of reflection entirely.

The questions you can ask yourself include:

1. What were you trying to accomplish? In retrospect, was this the best objective, or was there an alternative?
2. What strategy or approach did you plan to use to accomplish this? Would another approach have worked better?

3. What assumptions about yourself, others, or the situation were behind what you were trying to accomplish?

4. What actually happened? What did you do? How did others respond?

5. What were the results? How do these compare to your intended results?

6. What went well? What part did you play in this?

7. What didn't go well? What would you attribute that to?

8. What surprised you?

9. What was the biggest challenge? How did you handle it?

10. How did you practice [insert a skill you are trying to develop]?

11. What new possibilities do you now see?

12. What emotions are you experiencing as you reflect upon this experience?

13. What would you do differently next time?

14. What did you learn from this experience?

Three Levels of Learning

As you consider this list of questions, I want you to notice that some invite a deeper level of reflection than others. It's one thing to ask what happened and quite another to ask why it happened and still another to consider the deeper (rather than superficial) causes. A useful way of understanding this distinction comes from Bill Torbert, author of *Action Inquiry: The Secret of Timely and Transforming Leadership*. Torbert describes three forms of learning, which he calls "single loop," "double loop," and "triple loop":[52]

- *Single loop learning:* you respond by changing your behaviors. One question that prompts such learning is "What would you do differently next time?"

- *Double loop learning:* you respond by changing the strategies that lay behind these behaviors. A question you can ask here is "Would another approach have worked better?"

- *Triple loop learning:* you respond by changing the deeper purpose or intention that underlies those strategies. You ask, "What were you trying to accomplish" or, on a deeper level, "What assumptions were behind what you were trying to accomplish?"

This is similar to the Five Whys practice pioneered by Toyota to explore the cause-and-effect patterns behind problems or errors.[53] In both cases, you don't accept superficial explanations for what has happened. You look deeper. The main difference is that whereas the Five Whys typically sticks to behavioral causes, this learning model challenges you to also consider cognitive and emotional causes.

Assessing Progress in Reflecting

Let's say you begin to incorporate reflection into your day-to-day life. If you're the kind of person who likes to have indicators of progress, you may find yourself asking a question that my clients often put to me: "How do I know I'm getting better at reflecting?"

Now, if you're actually asking yourself this question, you *must* be making progress because you care enough to want to know. To this I say: kudos!

More practically, I like to distinguish three broad stages through which you progress as you build competence at reflection:

1. *No reflection.* You simply move from one action to the next without awareness of what happened or what you can do differently. At the very best, when things go wrong, you see how others, not you, can change.

2.   *Reflection after action.* You can look back after the fact, observe your behaviors, and consider what you can do differently.

3.   *Reflection in the midst of action.* You can simultaneously behave and observe yourself behaving. Your awareness is in two places at the same time—not easy to accomplish! This is sometimes known as self-observation.

For many years, I asked leaders to reflect in the midst of action. This was never easy for folks. Often, despite their best efforts, it simply didn't happen. The reasons for this remained a mystery to me until I came across research on the stages of development that adults progress through long after their bodies have stopped growing. It turns out that the mind you have at age 55 may not be the same mind you have at age 35. It can be qualitatively different, namely by having a greater capacity to handle complexity and reflect back upon itself. This is not guaranteed to happen, but it *can* happen.

In fact, it doesn't happen for all managers, or all adults, and herein lies the reason many managers have difficulty reflecting. Studies show that approximately 55 percent of managers fall into what I'm calling the *no reflection* category. If and when they look back on what happened, they are unable to see how their own behaviors played a role in negative results. Forty percent of managers are able to do *reflection after action*. Most of this group can see what they might do differently (*single loop learning*) but not why (*double* or *triple loop learning*). Less than 5 percent of managers are able to *reflect in the midst of action*, and of those who can, only a fraction do it consistently.[54]

The upshot of this research is important yet relatively simple: teach people to walk before they run, and don't expect miracles when repeated incremental progress is what matters. So although I still give people "self-observation exercises," my request to them is to pause after action (like at lunch or at the end of the day) to reflect. The measure of success then becomes how consistently they actually follow through and do this reflection. Once or twice a day is a reasonable standard.

Once you build a practice of reflecting, you start to notice all the habits that have been with you for years but were below your level of awareness. The way you habitually act in whatever area you are focusing on (e.g. arguing, telling stories, listening, asking questions) becomes an object in your awareness. As this happens, not only do you start calling B.S. on yourself, but you also start to wonder, "How do I know I'm making progress in becoming more aware of these habits?"

The 360 degree interviews that are part of most coaching engagements provide a reasonably good way to measure this, but they typically happen only once or twice a year. And not everyone has a coach. So I offer the following three metrics that, while not technically measurable, provide a distinction that you may find conceptually useful:

- When you engage in an old habit (e.g. interrupting others, losing your temper, speaking in a confusing way), what percentage of the time do you catch yourself doing this? Ten percent of the time? Half the time? It takes a long time to even get near 100 percent, but higher is always better.

- How long after the old habit occurs do you catch yourself? A minute? An hour? Two weeks? Progress means gradually shortening this amount of time.

- Of the occasions you catch yourself in an old habit, what percentage of the time do you self-correct by instituting new behaviors? Again, it takes a long time to even get close to 100 percent, but higher is better.

Now, let's say you become a superstar at reflecting on your own behaviors and the motivations behind them. This is an extraordinary feat worth celebrating. I would say "take yourself out to dinner," except that it's likely your colleagues will be so happy by the quality of your leadership that they'll take you out to dinner. When this happens, amidst the celebration and adulation, you may find yourself wondering, *How do I know my own reflective observations are accurate? What if others see something very different from me?* Your celebratory dinner isn't the time to ask these questions, but it does point toward the fourth and final step in the on-the-job practice cycle: getting feedback.

GETTING FEEDBACK

Leadership researchers tell us that one of the biggest differentiators between companies that have great leadership pipelines and those that don't is that the former give leaders large and rich amounts of feedback.[55]

The reason for this is rather simple: we need each other. We need each other to be able to see reality not just from one angle, but from many angles. We need each other to illuminate our blind spots so that what was previously hidden becomes visible.

High quality feedback does this. It provides what even the best reflection cannot: a multi-faceted perspective on a highly complex reality. Doing this helps rising stars avoid derailment. It prevents their Achilles Heels from becoming Achilles Hell. This is why companies with the best leadership pipelines provide large amounts of quality feedback.

Yet such companies are the exception. Most organizational cultures are either feedback-poor or feedback-predatory. Either you hear nothing of value or you get attacked. Silence or violence. Why is this the case?

Asking for, giving, and receiving feedback are as emotionally difficult as they are logistically simple. When you watch "feedback pros" do this, it looks easy and effortless. In many cases, it is, but only because they've done it a thousand times. You've done it twice. Not a fair comparison!

When you try *asking* for feedback yourself, a broad array of emotional barriers get in the way. Fear of rejection. Regret about what you've done. Embarrassment at placing yourself in the "inferior" role of asking for feedback. And a myriad of other emotions, each matched with an uncomfortable physical sensation.

When you think of *giving* feedback, even when asked, you face the realization that you risk violating the tacit agreements you've made with your colleagues: *If you say nice things to me, then I'll say nice things to you.* There is a reason you've made such agreements: you fear that if you are honest with your colleague, they will be more candid with you. And you're not sure you want that! Tacit agreements preserve the veneer of collegiality yet sacrifice the learning you get from each other's perspectives.

In paranoid cultures, the situation is even stickier. Shaming and blaming are so endemic that there is reasonable cause for you to feel afraid of asking for feedback and reluctant to give it. If you ask for it, you're likely to get hammered. If you give it, odds are good the other person will respond defensively and even retaliate by sending a bit of "feedback" (not the good kind) back your way.

Ironically, giving and receiving quality feedback is precisely the "medicine" that your organization needs to improve its health. Here's why: good feedback shows you with great precision exactly when you are practicing possibility leadership—and when you are not. No matter which practices you have taken on, quality feedback provides the best indicator of your progress or lack thereof.

What Constitutes High Quality Feedback?

Assuming you're ready to receive more feedback, how do you ensure that it produces the results you desire, namely more learning coupled with stronger relationships? What, indeed, constitutes high quality feedback? In my experience, high quality means specific, requested, ongoing, and real time feedback from a rich variety of competent observers. Let's break this definition down into its component parts so that you can guide others to give you such feedback:

- *Specific.* This means describing visibly observable behaviors. "You raised your voice and clenched your fist" is specific. "You got angry" is not. Such visible behaviors can include your words, body language, facial expression, tone of voice, etc. We can also distinguish specific feedback by its relevance to the particular skill you are practicing. If you are deliberately practicing how to ask great questions, getting feedback about this would be more useful than, say, feedback about the quality of the stories you tell.

- *Requested.* Your colleagues likely feel more comfortable giving their perspectives when you have asked for it and when they are confident that you will listen to them, take their words seriously, and not argue. You request it by saying, "I'd like to get your feedback about how well I asked questions in this afternoon's meeting. All I will do when you give feedback is listen, take notes, and ask clarifying questions." To make this promise credible, you have to follow through. No counter-arguments disguised as questions. Breathing deeply, feeling your feet on the ground, and posturing always help.

- *Ongoing.* Far too many organizations rely on annual performance reviews to tell people how they're doing. Once a year isn't enough, particularly for powerful senior executives who can get caught in bubbles because the only people who feel safe giving them feedback, their bosses, are either too busy or not competent at doing so. Here is a better standard: get feedback at least three times a week from three different sources.

- *Real time.* When I shadow senior managers (follow them around and observe them in action), I like to give them feedback immediately after observing them. The experience is fresh in their memory, and it's fresh in mine. I do this by contracting with them to have a conversation during the small "breaks" in the day. How can you do this if you don't have a coach shadowing you? Ask a trusted colleague to observe a particular behavior during a particular meeting and then give you 60 seconds of feedback in the hallway afterwards or through a short email that same day.

- *Rich variety.* The leadership research suggests that feedback works best when it comes from multiple people who see you in a range of contexts. An executive working on how well she listens might ask a direct report at the end of a 30 minute one on one meeting, "How well do you think I listened to you in this meeting? What could I do better?" Notice how different this is from asking a peer to provide feedback on her listening behaviors in a wide ranging strategic discussion involving twenty people. Both can be revealing, and the combination of the two can produce robust insights.

- *Competent observers.* I've conducted hundreds of 360 degree interviews over the years, and I've noticed that some people are much more skillful at observing people than others. I like to ask, "Can you give me a specific example of what so-and-so did or said? Can you tell me what you observed on their face or in their body language?" Some people provide nuanced details. Others have difficulty providing anything beyond vague adjectives. Many are in between. This makes it challenging to find competent observers, but some are better than none.

The standard for feedback is so low that I like to nudge leaders to stretch beyond what's comfortable. When they demur, I like to say, "If you think this is scary, let me tell about the time I called up six ex-girlfriends and asked them what they thought about me as a boyfriend and what they wished I had done differently." Yes, I have walked this path myself and can attest that a curious mind that musters the courage to ask unusual questions can experience profound learning.

Chapter 24

Seeking Out Challenge

I'M A FAN of changing from where you are today rather than lunging after a new job, relationship, or city in a belief it will make you more content or effective. That's why I haven't said anything yet in this book about whether your current job is "the right job" for you at this point in time and, if not, what else might be. I've been more interested in helping you develop yourself *within* your current situation. As we've seen, deciding what parts of possibility leadership to practice and learning how to practice them can improve the quality of your leadership by freeing you to bring your best.

Now it's time to talk at a higher level of altitude about the actual nature of your work. Here are two reasons why:

1. No matter how you approach your current role as it is now defined (and no matter how well you practice new skills), it may not give you the challenges you need to be fully engaged and

rising to your best. Either you've mastered the challenges of the role, or it was never a great stretch for you from the outset.

2. The leadership development research tells us that some experiences are better at producing leadership competence than others. Not all jobs are created equal, and not all ways of scoping a job are equally effective at building the particular kinds of competence your organization needs its future leaders to possess. In other words, even if you're not lacking in challenge, are you encountering the "right" challenges, the ones that will teach you the skills you need to learn?

This brings me to back to the research done by the Center for Creative Leadership over thirty years ago and updated in the past decade. The same researchers who described what negative behaviors can derail leaders also discovered what activities can accelerate their development. In extensive interviews with successful executives, they asked these executives what experiences had shaped them the most. You may not be surprised to hear that the vast preponderance of learning happened through on-the-job experience, not formal training. But the researchers learned something else that may come as news to you: there is a distinct set of experiences that teach leadership lessons better than others. The original study listed 17 experiences.[56] The updated study, which looked at African American and women leaders (as compared to the original study of white men), added six for a total of 23 experiences.[57] Here are five that stand out to me:

- Starting from scratch
- Turnarounds
- Increased scope
- Line-to-staff switch
- Special bosses (very good or very bad)

According to CCL researchers, these five experiences and the rest on their list tend to produce more and better learning for the leaders who have them. As you look at the list, you may be thinking, "Well, of course." But is this how your organization is developing its leaders? Does the leadership conversation focus on the pivotal experiences and who will make the most of them, or does it revolve around a seemingly robust yet amorphous set of "competencies?" When senior managers hire people, do they ask themselves, "Which up-and-coming leaders can learn the most from this experience so they'll be ready for bigger roles?" Or do they simply hire the most qualified person who may or may not learn the lessons the experience teaches and therefore may or may not be propelled to future success at more senior levels? Needless to say, there is an enormous difference between these two sets of criteria. (And by the way, I'm not advocating for hiring solely based on who learns best. Good hiring managers consider both performance *and* learning credentials. They also assess the risk and cost of failure of hiring somebody who is not 100 percent ready for the role.)

What does this mean for you? Here is a series of questions for you to ask, hopefully in conversation with your manager and possibly in collaboration with a strategic HR leader:

1. What is the uppermost role you could potentially be hired for?
2. To succeed in this role, what lessons (about the business, about managing, etc?) will you need to have learned from prior experiences?
3. Which of these lessons can you learn from your existing role as currently defined?
4. Which can you not?
5. What combination of new experiences now and in coming years will teach you the additional lessons you need to learn?
6. How can you build these challenging experiences into your existing role? By redefining the role? By taking on a special

assignment, joining a task force, or participating on an action learning team?

7. When will it be time to move to a different position?

8. What support structures—like feedback, in-the-moment coaching from your manager, reflective time, support from an external coach, or training that matches your skill focus—can you receive to maximize what you learn from these experiences?

Unless you work for one of the organizations that are true "talent machines," I'll bet good money that nobody has asked you these questions before. Maybe the one about uppermost role, but not the others. So I applaud you for simply being willing to bring these into your field of awareness.

Now, I want to point out two pieces of good news about seeking out challenges. First, building your leadership development strategy around on-the-job experience (among other things) already makes a lot of sense to you—and to your manager and your manager's manager. It's how you assume you have always learned best, right? And so it's likely to be something you're willing to sign up for in the future. The "club" of on-the-job-learning requires no new membership, just the renewal of your existing membership. Second, you probably prefer it to the sophisticated-sounding yet vague language of competencies or the option of heading off to a course that may or may not relate to what you're learning on the job. So, when I encourage you to seek out challenges on the job, I trust that you find this to be a welcome proposition.

CHAPTER 25

TOWARD A WAY OF BEING

THIS BOOK STARTED rather unusually with a defense of paranoia as a selective mindset. I'd like to end it with three stories that illustrate the value of possibility leadership as a permanent way of living:

Drew (a composite of two people) has been a senior manager for twenty years. He is known for accomplishing big things, staying positive, and giving polished presentations. He works hard and is proud of his feats. However, interviews reveal that most people who work with him feel like they don't really know him and wonder about his sincerity. *Is this what he really feels or is this just for show?* This assessment hits Drew hard, but after significant reflection he acknowledges that he actually doesn't know what he's feeling most of the time, so how could others? This suppression of feeling is a direct expression of his Achilles Heel. After three months of observing his own emotions and learning the language of emotion (sadness, fear, contentment, disgust, delight, etc.), he starts to practice a new way of speaking. To be specific, he starts to practice speaking authentically, which includes revealing what he is feeling. He also begins to listen more deeply to others. Neither practice is easy—after all, he is a beginner at this emotional stuff—but over time he gets the hang of it and even starts to enjoy it.

How do others respond? At first, they're not sure what to think. *Drew sure is acting strangely.* But when they see this behavior show up more consistently, they begin to appreciate it—and trust him. *I really know where he's coming from. He feels real.* As others develop greater trust in Drew's sincerity, they sign on wholeheartedly to his big visions.

Gina (also a composite) is a bright 40-something leader in a Fortune 100 company with great potential. Her greatest asset is discernment. She can pinpoint what's missing in a plan or strategy and suggest how to improve it. She also takes care of her staff and is widely respected for her competence and integrity. Yet, like Drew, she has an Achilles Heel. Instead of sincerity, her issue is appreciation. It is not uncommon for her to publicly criticize others' ideas and even disparage them as individuals. This is particularly true with peers, several of whom tell me she has an "attitude" and is "hard to work with because you never know what she's going to say about you." When hearing this assessment, Gina readily agrees that it sounds like her. On a deeper level, we discover that the voice inside her head that can be critical of others is actually brutal toward herself. This "inner critic" is part pit bull, part sniper, and always on the attack.

After observing it in action for a few weeks, she takes on two new practices: keeping a list of what she is grateful for that day (a sly way of calling B.S. on her critical mind) and doing a physical movement that makes her body more flexible (and improves her posturing). Over time, these practices quiet her inner critic and help her accept others' flaws and mistakes. She "neutral"izes two key relationships that were on the rocks and builds a more positive public identity in the company.

In 1997 *Shawn Green* (his real name, but not someone I've coached) was a talented Major League Baseball player who was frustrated by being benched. Not only that, but after a confrontation with the team's batting coach, he was prohibited from going to the batting cage without the coach's supervision—an insulting restriction. Rather than sulk in resentment and resignation, Shawn started a new practice. He found a batting tee and net in a little-used area outside the clubhouse and started hitting by himself. (Batting tees are decidedly *not* how pros practice.) He visualized game situations and pretended that "I was facing all of the pitchers I was currently being forced to watch from the dugout...[and] notice[d] the sound of the ball swishing against the back net." His mind quieted and his breathing became "rhythmic." He repeated this batting meditation every day.

In his first at bat after being placed in the lineup, he hit a home run against the All-Star pitcher, Greg Maddux. Within a month, his batting average had increased by sixty points. At first teammates teased him about traveling with a tee, but over time they gained respect for this unorthodox practice. In the coming years, he added other deliberate practices like improving his stride by "imagining with my foot and shoulder" and anticipating pitches by carefully watching individual pitchers and keeping a journal of their patterns. The result? A fifteen-year career with a lifetime .280 batting average and over 300 home runs, including four homers in a single game (a record).[58]

As someone biologically wired more for negative than positive emotion, I find stories like these to be inspiring. They challenge me to live and lead with my best stuff even when the odds are stacked against me. And they remind me that just as possibility leadership inevitably requires an encounter with paranoia, the path to great leadership winds through the valley of risk and awkwardness. This is because:

• The practices that evoke excellence are unusual and often uncomfortable—at least at first.

- These practices are also uncommon and can look "weird." Others may have negative judgments about them. So may you.

- An effective set of practices shifts your outer behaviors while simultaneously growing your inner experiences into healthier and more mature forms.

- When you select practices wisely and practice them deliberately, the results speak for themselves. Others' negative judgment morphs into respect, and your own discomfort shifts into pride that you are leading at your best.

Enjoy the practicing and drop me a line to let me know how it's going.

Notes

[1] Kegan, Robert and L. Laskow Lahey. *Immunity to Change: How to Overcome It and Unlock the Potential in Yourself and Your Organization.* Boston: Harvard Business Press, 2009, p. 49.

[2] My classmate is now a venture capitalist in Silicon Valley.

[3] Lewis, Thomas, F. Amini and R. Lannon. *A General Theory of Love.* New York, NY: Vintage Books, 2001.

[4] Criminal activity and rule-breaking are real. Healthy control systems discourage people from doing "bad things" and catch them before they can do real damage. Knowing that such systems are in place gives line managers trust that they might not otherwise have. This is why competent internal and external auditors, for example, can promote possibility leadership.

[5] See for example Gallup's 2012 study *Engagement at Work: Its Effect on Performance Continues in Tough Economic Times.* Available on www.gallup.com

[6] Rock, David. "Managing with the Brain in Mind." *Strategy + Business.* Autumn 2009.

[7] Boudreau, John W. (2010-07-01). "Retooling HR: Using Proven Business Tools to Make Better Decisions About Talent" (Kindle Locations 437-440). *Harvard Business Review Press.* Kindle Edition.

[8] Eichenwald, Kurt. "Microsoft's Lost Decade." *Vanity Fair,* August 2012.

[9] Pink, Daniel. *Drive: The Surprising Truth About What Motivates Us.* New York, NY: Riverhead Books, 2009.

[10] These numbers are estimates used to make a point rather than statistically valid figures.

[11] Schwartz, Tony. *Be Excellent at Anything: The Four Keys to Transforming the Way We Work and Live.* New York, NY: Free Press, 2010, p. 67.

[12] Grove, Andrew. *Only the Paranoid Survive: How to Exploit the Crisis Points That Challenge Every Company.* New York, NY: Currency, 1996, p. 123.

[13] Grove, *Only the Paranoid Survive,* p. 110.

[14] Grove, *Only the Paranoid Survive,* p. 119.

[15] Grove, *Only the Paranoid Survive,* p. 119.

[16] Some have cited Gilligan's *In A Different Voice* as evidence that women, unlike men, are not hierarchical. However, her research suggests that although women are more likely than men to *think* non-hierarchically, they *develop* through successive hierarchical stages, each more inclusive than the prior one.

[17] Grove, *Only the Paranoid Survive*, pp. 89-90.

[18] For the full story, you'll have to wait for my next book, tentatively titled *The Purple Couch and Other Leadership Lessons from a Decade of Dating*.

[19] Gottman, John M. *The Relationship Cure: A 5 Step Guide to Strengthening Your Marriage, Family and Friendships*. New York, NY: Three Rivers Press, 2001.

[20] This is not a typo. Gottman's research shows that the fastest way to end a relationship is to turn *away from* the other person's bids.

[21] Quoted in Dahle, Cheryl. "What Are You Complaining About?" *Fast Company*, May 2001.

[22] I am taking the liberty to use Gottman's phrases in the context of responding to complaints. These applications are mine, not his.

[23] Kegan, Robert and L.Lahey. *How The Way We Talk Can Change the Way We Work: Seven Languages for Transformation*. San Francisco: Jossey-Bass, 2002.

[24] Marshall, Lisa. *Speak The Truth and Point to Hope: The Leader's Journey to Maturity*. Dubuque, Iowa: Kendall/Hunt, 2004.

[25] "A Conversation on Leadership with Carol and Jack Weber." *Virginia Business*, July 2007.

[26] Founder of New Ventures West. See his book *Coaching: Evoking Excellence in Others*. Boston: Butterworth Heinemann, 1999.

[27] Brownell, Judi. *Fostering Service Excellence Through Listening*. The Center for Hospitality Research, Cornell University, 2009.

[28] I have adapted this list of listening filters from a model of personal development called the Enneagram.

[29] Mintzberg, Henry, B. Ahlstrand and J. Lampel. *Strategy Bites Back: It Is Far More And Less Than You Ever Imagined*. Upper Saddle River, NJ: Pearson Prentice Hall, 2005.

[30] For a summary of the original BCG case and Pascale's findings, see Mintzberg, Henry, B. Ahlstrand and J. Lampel. *Strategy Safari: A Guided Tour Through The Wilds of Strategic Management*. New York, NY: Free Press, 1998.

[31] Siegel, Daniel. *Mindsight: The New Science of Personal Transformation*. New York, NY: Bantam Books, 2011.

[32] McCall, Morgan. "The Experience Conundrum." *Harvard Business Press Chapters*, 2010.

[33] Riso, Don R. and R. Hudson. *Personality Types: Using the Enneagram for Self-Discovery*. Boston: Houghton Mifflin, 1996.

[34] www.hoganassessments.com

[35] Hogan, Joyce, R. Hogan and R. Kaiser. *Management Derailment: Personality Assessment and Mitigation*. downloaded from hoganassessments.com

[36] Seligman, Martin. *Authentic Happiness. Using the New Positive Psychology to Realize Your Potential for Lasting Fulfillment*. New York, NY: Atria, 2003.

[37] Argyris, Chris. *Overcoming Organizational Defenses*. New York, NY: Prentice Hall, 1990.

[38] Allen, David. *Getting Things Done: The Art of Stress-Free Productivity*. New York, NY: Penguin, 2002.

[39] Remind me to include this on the list of powerful questions in the next edition of this book.

[40] Mintzberg, Henry. *Managing*. New York, NY: Berrett-Koehler, 2009.

[41] Quoted in Tony Schwartz's book *Be Excellent at Anything*.

[42] www.jordangruber.com/rebound

[43] I first encountered this concept in Shawn Phillips's *Strength for Life*.

[44] Buettner, Dan. *Blue Zones: Lessons For Living Longer From The People Who've Lived The Longest*. Washington DC: National Geographic, 2010.

[45] Schwartz, Tony. *Be Excellent At Anything*.

[46] Schwartz, Tony. *Be Excellent At Anything*.

[47] www.seanleclaire.com

[48] Jim and John Harbaugh, who coached against each other in the 2013 Super Bowl, both send game film each week to their father, Jack Harbaugh, a former college coach. Every Tuesday, Jack watches both films in case either son calls to get his perspective. Source: *The Herd with Colin Cowherd*, ESPN Radio, June 14, 2013.

[49] Colvin, Geoff. *Talent Is Overrated: What Really Separates World-Class Performers From Everybody Else*. New York, NY: Portfolio Trade, 2010.

[50] Quoted in Mintzberg's book *Managing*. The original study appeared in Mintzberg's first book, *The Nature of Managerial Work* (1973).

[51] Mintzberg, Henry. *Managing*.

[52] Torbert, William. *Action Inquiry: The Secret of Timely and Transforming Leadership*. San Francisco: Berrett-Koehler, 2004.

[53] The Five Whys is part of the Toyota Production System or "lean" management. For applications of lean, look at Mark Graban's blog

(www.leanblog.org). For a strategic perspective, check out *The Hitchhiker's Guide to Lean* by Jamie Flinchbaugh and Andy Carlino.

[54] Joiner, Bill and S. Josephs. *Leadership Agility: Five Levels of Mastery for Anticipating and Initiating Change.* San Francisco: Wiley, 2007.

[55] Charan, Ram & B. Conaty. *The Talent Masters: Why Smart Leaders Put People Before Numbers.* New York, NY: Random House, 2011.

[56] McCall, Morgan, M. Lombardo and A. Morrison. *The Lessons of Experience: How Successful Executives Develop on the Job.* New York, NY: Lexington Books, 1988, pg. 10.

[57] Douglas, Christina. *Key Events and Lessons for Managers in a Diverse Workforce.* Greensboro, NC: Center for Creative Leadership, 2003.

[58] Greene, Shawn. *The Way of Baseball: Finding Stillness at 95 MPH.* New York, NY: Simon & Schuster, 2011.

Acknowledgements

I am deeply grateful to the many managers who have invited me into their lives as their coach, whether for three months or three years. It is an incredible honor.

This is my first book, so I thank several other *firsts*:

- Frank H., the first person I coached; Doug S., the first person I coached for an extended period of time; Kathy Burke, the first person who coached me; and Pam Weiss, Sarita Chawla, and James Flaherty, my first and best coaching teachers.

- Mike Cohen, my first true adult best friend; Jon Rubenstein and Michael Dolan for being first to JAM; Simon Turkalj for being the first person I turn to for creative provocation; Steve March for first showing me what a real book collection looks like; Bill Hefferman for first modeling how to use a strengths-based approach in a big company; Janet Crawford for first showing me the connection between brain science and leadership; and Raleigh Woods for first teaching me how to argue about sports and politics with gusto and humor.

As I think about the professional opportunities in my life, I feel gratitude for the following people:

- Ed O'Neil and Rob Williams, who took a chance on a 22-year-old and launched a career.
- Stacy Flaherty, who brought me into the center of New Ventures West's wonderful community.

- Donna Fowler, Dana Brenner-Kelly, Julie Rubinstein, Cy Hufano, Lori Emerick, Mariann Pike, Lynette Winter, Jennifer Wallace, Rand Schenck, and Kristen Krull, all of who made pivotal connections that allowed me to serve more leaders.
- Cindy Becker, who trusted me to help transform a public sector organization from the inside.
- Jeannie Coyle, who re-introduced me to the CCL research, and Jan Carothers of NSA Oregon, who encouraged me to write.

My intellectual forebears are tall and numerous:

- Ken Wilber, Bill Torbert, Robert Kegan, Lisa Lahey, Susanne Cook-Greuter, Bill Joiner, Stephen Josephs, Sean Hargens, Jennifer Garvey-Berger, and others who have advanced integral and constructivist adult developmental theory.
- Russ Hudson and Don Riso, whose approach to the Enneagram pervades everything I do.
- James Flaherty for giving me a learning curriculum that will keep me busy for the next few decades.
- Fernando Flores, Chauncey Bell, Matthew Budd, Tracy Goss, Alan Sieler, and other practitioners of speech acts, language, and conversations.
- Martin Seligman, Marcus Buckingham, Donald Clifton, John Gottman, Tom Rath, Mihaly Csikszentmaihalyi, Sonya Lyubomirsky, Robert Quinn, Jane Dutton, and other thought leaders in positive psychology and the strengths-based school of leadership development.
- Henry Mintzberg for offering a dynamic and integrative understanding of strategy.
- Art Kleiner, whose books about corporate heretics and core groups remind me of what's possible and why it's so hard.
- Tony Schwartz, Shawn Phillips, Jerzy and Aniela Gregorek, Jonny Bowden, Christine Caldwell, Rob Wolf, and Tim Ferriss for

influencing my understanding of health, nutrition, sleep, and physical energy.

I thank Elizabeth Fausnight for skilled copy editing and Shoshana Rosenfeld for sound advice on branding.

Oh… did I mention I have an amazing family?

- My four wonderful parents, who have each contributed something special to my life, Larry and Joanne Handelsman and Wendy and Phil Baia.
- My brother, Alex, who introduced me to the Paleo diet and challenged me to write a book *now*.
- My sister, Valerie, for the guidance about mud masks and living life with zest.
- My aunt, Linda Handelsman, for introducing me to the virtues of dark chocolate.
- My sister- and brother-in-law, Wendy Endress and Bill Livingston, who have hosted me countless times on business trips up to Tacoma and Seattle.
- My sons, Jacob and Zander, who never cease to delight and intrigue me.

Last but not least, thank you, Julie, for supporting this project—and me—with love and patience.